OSPREY
MILITARY

CAMPAIGN SERIES 2

AUSTERLITZ 1805

Austerlitz – the late battle, after Vernet. In the centre foreground a disconsolate group of prisoners from the Tsar's Chevalier Guard are led towards Napoleon (right), while in the distance, beyond the Pratzen, Marshal Bernadotte's I Corps advances in line against the collapsing Austro-Russian centre.

On the extreme right centre, French artillery opens fire on the hapless Allied left, now trapped around the Satschan ponds, and French gun-teams advance at the gallop to reinforce their colleagues. (Anne S. K. Brown Military Collection, Brown University)

GENERAL EDITOR DAVID G. CHANDLER

OSPREY MILITARY

CAMPAIGN SERIES 2

AUSTERLITZ 1805

BATTLE OF THE THREE EMPERORS

DAVID G. CHANDLER

This book is dedicated to my friends and comrades of the Napoleonic Association of Great Britain.

The passage of the Danube near Vienna, by Chavane after Siméon Fort. The capture intact of the Tabor Bridge at Vienna on 13 November 1805 by the French was a celebrated coup. Prince Murat, Marshal Lannes and General Bertrand bluffed the Austrian defenders into believing that an armistice had been signed, and then promptly took possession of the bridge. This brazen act secured Napoleon a major crossing-place over the Danube. (Anne S. K. Brown Military Collection, Brown University)

First published in Great Britain in 1990 by Osprey, an imprint of Reed Consumer Books Limited Michelin House, 81 Fulham Road London SW3 6RB and Auckland, Melbourne, Singapore and Toronto

Reprinted 1992, 1993

Wargaming Austerlitz by Arthur Harman.
Wargames consultant Duncan Macfarlane.

British Library Cataloguing in Publication Data
Chandler, David, *1934–*
Austerlitz 1805; the battle of the three emperors. – (Osprey campaign series, 2)
1. Napoleonic Wars. Battle of Austerlitz
1. Title
940.2'7
ISBN 1-85045-957-5

Produced by DAG Publications Ltd for Osprey Publishing Ltd.
Colour bird's eye view illustrations by Cilla Eurich.
Cartography by Micromap.
Typeset by Ronset Typesetters Ltd, Darwen, Lancashire.
Mono camerawork by M&E. Reproductions, North Fambridge, Essex.
Printed and bound in Hong Kong.

CONTENTS

THE ROAD TO WAR IN 1805

The first step on the long road that was ultimately to lead to the Battle of Austerlitz was taken late on 14 March 1804, when a party of French dragoons commanded by *Général de Brigade* Michel Ordener violated the neutral territory of Baden to seize Louis Antoine Henri de Bourbon-Condé, Duc d'Enghien, at the town of Ettenheim. This French prince – related to the exiled royal house of Bourbon – was escorted to the forbidding Château de Vincennes outside Paris, courtmartialled on charges of treason, and shot before dawn in the moat on the 21st. This ruthless act had been authorized by Napoleon Bonaparte, currently Consul-for-Life of the French Republic, to serve as a dire warning to his enemies that he would treat plots against his person with the utmost severity. 'It was more than a crime; it was a mistake', opined Minister of Police, Joseph Fouché. Whatever the truth of that, this execution of a Bourbon princeling was destined to expedite a series of events that would reach their dramatic climax amid the frosty hillsides and fields of distant Moravia on 2 December 1805.

The execution of the Prince did not lead to any immediate declaration of war against France, but the repugnance it caused in St Petersburg, Vienna and Berlin helped doom the general peace that had existed on the continent of Europe since the signature of the Peace of Lunéville in February 1801. In fact the state of peace was already wearing decidedly thin as George III had already unilaterally resumed war against France as early as May 1803. Clashes of interest with France in the West Indies, the Mediterranean and south-east Europe had led to the resumption of naval warfare barely 14 months after the signature of the Peace of Amiens, but Napoleon's arbitrary act in March 1804 helped to prepare the way for the development of a general European conflagration once more. It undoubtedly hastened the formation of the Third Coalition – an alliance that Prime Minister William Pitt the Younger strove hard to achieve upon his return to office in May 1804. After months of intensive negotiations, a series of treaties were signed on 11 April 1805 (effective from 9 August) uniting Great Britain, Russia and Austria in a formidable league – at least on paper – which would be further strengthened when and if a vacillating Prussia made up its mind to join. Napoleon, having 'sown the wind' might well appear to have been about to 'reap the whirlwind'.

In fact this unfavourable development came as no great surprise to Napoleon, decreed as Emperor of the French on 18 May 1804 and crowned as such at Notre Dame the following 2 December. During the Consulate he had once stated that 'Between old monarchies and a young republic a spirit of hostility must always exist. In the present state of affairs every peace treaty means no more than a brief armistice: and I believe that my destiny will be to fight almost continuously.' Secure in his relationship with his adopted French populace, and serenely confident in his abilities, Napoleon gave not a fig for the innate hostility of Hanoverian, Romanov, Habsburg or Hohenzollern ruling houses. That a new struggle lay ahead was certain in his mind; his coronation as King of Italy in May 1805 was a further challenge to their over-developed sense of royal propriety; the only real questions were exactly when and where the general conflagration would break out.

Preparations for Wider War

By mid-1804, Napoleon had already prepared the weapon he would need to destroy any new hostile coalition – namely what was soon to be called *la Grande Armée*. The years of peace had also helped him expedite the reorganization of France's economy, political organization and system of laws

– embodied in the famous Codes – but it was the creation of a truly united French army and navy over the same period that represented his most important achievement. 'Once we had the Army of Italy, of Germany and of Switzerland. Now we have only a single army – and soon we shall see it in action.' Organized into self-contained *corps d'armée*, commanded by newly-created Marshals of the Empire such as Ney, Lannes, Soult and Davout, the army had been provided with a prolonged training period at the Camp of Boulogne.

From the autumn of 1803 until August 1805, the greater part of the army's strength was deployed along, or within range of, the north-eastern coasts of France. Determined to invade 'Perfidious Albion' as soon as naval considerations in *La Manche* would allow, Napoleon had ordered the formation of large encampments at Moulin-Hubert near Boulogne, at Etaples and Ambleteuse, St Omer and Bruges, eventually capable of containing over 150,000 men. The neighbouring ports were packed with barges, gunboats and two-masted *prames*.

The long series of delays in launching the invasion of England were in large measure blamed on the French fleet and its commanders. To secure the crossing of the Channel it was vital that the Royal Navy should be drawn away far to the

The Camps of Boulogne, unattributed sketch. The largest camp near Moulin-Hubert, occupied between 1803 and 1805, soon took on the appearance of a small town. Soldiers were encouraged to decorate their huts and to cultivate gardens. (Anne S. K. Brown Military Collection, Brown University Library)

The distribution of Crosses of the Legion of Honour. On 16 August 1804, Napoleon awarded the first mass distribution of the Legion of Honour. The white enamel crosses on their watered-silk red ribbons became highly prized and much sought-after. As Napoleon once remarked, 'It is with baubles that men are led.' (Anne S. K. Brown Military Collection, Brown University Library)

westwards for the critical period. Accordingly *Vice-Amiral* Villeneuve and a strong squadron slipped out of close-blockaded Toulon on 30 March 1805 and sailed for the West Indies. Once he had drawn off Lord Nelson in pursuit, his orders were to double back across the Atlantic, to raise the blockade of Brest, sail around Scotland to link with the Dutch fleet in the River Texel, and then to safeguard the army's passage to Pegwell Bay in Kent, the designated invasion point. At first this major operation went well. After collecting a Spanish squadron from Cadiz, Villeneuve arrived off Martinique on 4 June with 29 vessels, captured a fort, and then set off once more for Europe on the 9th. Vice-Admiral Lord Nelson, meanwhile, had duly fallen for the bait and set off in pursuit with the main British fleet, but failed to make contact with the elusive French.

So far, all was going according to Napoleon's master plan, but Villeneuve's audacity was fast diminishing. Arriving back in European waters, he was met by a small naval force under Admiral Calder off Cape Finisterre, and in a sharp but indecisive engagement lost two Spanish sail. After a sojourn in La Coruña, he moved on to Ferrol where another Spanish squadron joined him. Then on 4 August he sailed with 33 ships to raise the blockade of Brest – and then to head for Scotland. But hardly had he put to sea than he met with a neutral trading vessel whose master informed him (quite erroneously) that a large British fleet lay over the horizon blocking his path. Villeneuve decided it was too dangerous to proceed with Napoleon's intentions and sailed into the Spanish port of Cadiz on 20 August – where he was promptly blockaded by Nelson's returning squadrons.

The news of Villeneuve's unathorized arrival in Cadiz was passed by visual telegraph to Boulogne, where Napoleon was at his headquarters in the château of Pont de Briques. It is probable that he had already been considering abandoning the enterprise against England, as spy reports had already reached him indicating that Austria and Russia were preparing to take the field once more against France. Nevertheless, he seized upon Villeneuve's recent actions to blame the admiral for making the invasion of England impossible. On 25 August the definitive orders were issued, cancelling all the invasion preparations and calling into being *la Grande Armée d'Allemagne*. 'My mind is made up,' wrote Napoleon to his Foreign Minister, Talleyrand. 'My movement has begun. By 17 September I shall be with 200,000 men in Germany.'

This radical change of intention was carefully disguised. To fool the watchful Royal Navy frigates overlooking the coast, rear-parties lit bonfires in the encampments, and Napoleon himself lingered in the area until 3 September. But meanwhile his troops were marching for the Rhine (the Imperial Guard received orders dated 28th August to move to Strasbourg), as the first stage of a grand movement through Europe to threaten Vienna. Prophesying that Austria would be pacified 'before winter', Napoleon now envisaged a grandiose two-part plan. While Massena launched a major drive through North Italy towards the Alpine passes by way of a distraction, Napoleon at the head of seven corps intended to sweep through Germany from the Rhine to the Danube, there to seek a decisive battle against the Austrians before their Russian allies could appear in the theatre of war. Prussian intentions were as yet unclear – but Talleyrand's tempting offer of Hanover was enough to keep Frederick William III sitting on the fence, at least for the time being. Thus was set in train one of the most dramatic campaigns in modern history.

PLANS AND PREPARATIONS

The Plans of the Third Coalition

Prime Minister William Pitt's search for Continental allies against France had been greatly assisted by the d'Enghien incident already described. It cost Napoleon the admiring regard of the 27-year-old Tsar Alexander I, who had succeeded his father after a palace revolution in which the son was at least in part implicated, in 1801. Russia had been suspicious of French intentions in the Balkans and Mediterranean for some little time since making peace in late 1800, but the Tsar only began making cautious preparations for renewed war in mid-1804, opening overtures with Vienna with an alliance in view. The Habsburg Emperor, Francis II, proved none too eager initially, and a first, somewhat vague treaty was only signed on 4 November of that year. Next, putting aside disagreements with England over Turkey and Malta, Alexander's diplomats approached William Pitt – who was happy to oblige – and the resultant Convention of St Petersburg was signed on 11 April 1805. Thus the fundamentals of a new alliance had been achieved, especially after Austria came more firmly into line by signing full agreements on 16 July and 9 August later the same year, and it was anticipated that other German and Baltic states, and Bourbon Naples,

would soon accede. Prussia remained an enigma, but for the rest France was practically isolated – with only Bavaria and Württemberg, and French-dominated areas such as North Italy, Holland and Switzerland, available as friends.

The statesmen of the Third Coalition proceeded to draw up a grandiose master plan, comprising four connected offensives involving almost half a million men. Taking these projected offensives in turn from north to south, in the first place came the liberation of Hanover, and its restoration to its Elector, George III of Great Britain. For this purpose, 15,000 British troops were to be landed at Cuxhaven, aided by 12,000 Swedes and 20,000 Russians collecting at Stralsund. In time these forces might be joined by General Bennigsen's 50,000 Russians from Puklawi on the Vistula, and a further force being organized at Riga by Generals Buxhöwden and Michelson. These Russian armies would also serve to bring pressure to bear on the King of Prussia; his adherence to the alliance would be worth a further 200,000 men.

The Allies next turned their attention to Bavaria on the western Danube. This misguided ally of France was to be occupied by 85,000 Austrians under Quartermaster General Mack and the Archduke Ferdinand, joined in due time by General Kutusov at the head of 85,000 Russians. Together they would advance on the Rhine from Ulm. Linking the south German front with North Italy, the Archduke John with 25,000 Austrians was to occupy the Tyrol and the neighbouring Alpine passes, being prepared to operate northwards towards Ulm or southwards into Italy according to circumstances.

Northern Italy was considered to be the most likely scene for Napoleon's main riposte, considering the events of 1796/7 and 1800, and the fact that he had recently crowned himself King of

The Plans of the Third Alliance (strategic)

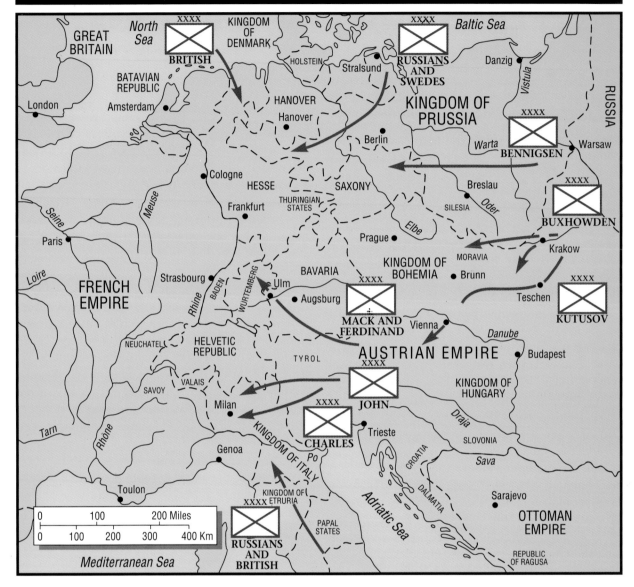

Italy. In this theatre, the gifted Archduke Charles was accordingly to command 100,000 of the finest Austrian troops, with orders to expel Viceroy Eugène Beauharnais (Napoleon's stepson) and regain Lombardy before invading the south of France. Further south again, a hybrid force of British (from Malta), 17,000 Russians and a force of Albanians, joined by 36,000 Bourbon troops from Sicily, were to reconquer Naples before advancing to cooperate with the Archduke Charles. They would be backed if necessary by more soldiers of the Tsar collecting at Odessa prior to advancing into the Balkan states of Moldavia and Wallachia. Finally, Great Britain agreed to find an amphibious force for raiding the coasts of France and Holland, and to help encourage a new Chouan revolt in Brittany and La Vendée on behalf of the exiled house of Bourbon.

All in all this amounted to a staggering plan of Europe-wide operations – at least on paper. How practicable it was to prove only time would tell. Problems of coordination would be immense – but such matters were brushed aside. It was not everywhere appreciated, for example, that the Russians were using a different calendar from the rest of Europe. On the difference of 12 days a great deal was going to depend.

Napoleon's Dispositions and Counter-Plans

Inevitably, French spies placed throughout Europe got wind of what was afoot. The overall picture was certainly daunting. To meet these complex machinations France could call upon some 250,000 trained troops and a further 150,000 newly-mobilized conscripts. In mid-August 1805, Marshal Bernadotte was occupying Hanover, Marmont was in Holland, Gouvion Saint Cyr in Naples and Jourdan commanding under Eugène in Piedmont. Most of the remaining troops were in the coastal camps of northern France, all of 730 miles from their threatened ally, Bavaria, whose ruler could call upon only some 20,000 soldiers and possibly a few Württembergers. Barely 100,000 men were available to protect the frontiers of France and her allies against the threat posed by at least 400,000 confederate troops. Even worse, French forward resources were grouped in four widely separated regions – in Hanover, Swabia, Piedmont and Naples.

How could the Coalition's threats be met and nullified? It was clear to Napoleon that he must at all costs seize the initiative and use the formations presently manning the Channel coast as the greater part of his pre-emptive offensive. Surprise, determination and a clear aim might help redress a great deal of his overall numerical disadvantage.

The selection of his main target was simplified by Allied delays in implementing even the preliminary stages of most of their grandiose plans. Only on the Danube front was anything resembling a target presenting itself by late September. On the 10th of that month, General Mack invaded Bavaria and later occupied the city of Ulm. This act – designed to punish French supporters and to block any French attempt to advance from the Rhine through the Black Forest – once and for all threw Bavaria into the French alliance and provided Napoleon with both a *casus belli* and a suitable target. Mack paused west of Ulm to await the arrival

of Kutusov, unaware that the Russians (keeping to their 'Old Style' system of dating) were in fact only just beginning to enter distant Moravia. Austrian intelligence had realized that some 30,000 French troops were moving towards Strasbourg – doubtless to strengthen the frontier defences in that area. For the rest, it appeared that the mass of French troops were still far away on the Channel coast. Austrian senior officers spoke bravely of soon carrying the war deep into France – even to the gates of Paris – and prophesied the rapid demise of the threat posed by the upstart French Empire.

They were destined to be very much surprised. Unbeknown to Vienna, Napoleon, his mind made up, was on the point of unleashing a devastating strategic offensive – taking the form of a great concentric wheel by seven *corps d'armée*, totalling over 200,000 men between them, advancing along separate but closely interrelated lines of march steadily converging on the Danube between Münster, Dönauwörth and Ingolstädt, with the intention of encircling and eliminating Mack's army before his Russian allies could make an effective appearance. Elsewhere, Massena with 50,000 men was to contain the Archduke Charles in North Italy, and Gouvion St Cyr was to defend Naples against attack. Only Marshal Brune, with 30,000 men, was left near the Channel to guard against any British sea-borne incursion. A great military epic was in the making – and beyond it would lie still greater achievements.

From the Rhine to the Danube

The first French formations left their Channel camps on 25 August; the last marched out on 3 September, the same day that Napoleon left for Paris, where a financial crisis had demanded his immediate attention. Meanwhile his major formations rapidly marched eastward to their designated forming-up places on or near the Rhine, the *Grande Armée*'s left wing – moving from Hanover and Utrecht – was to rendezvous in Württemberg. The centre and right (the troops from the Channel) were to take post along the middle Rhine at Mannheim, Spire, Lauterburg and Strasbourg. Murat's cavalry rode ahead for the last-named city, with orders to mount diversionary

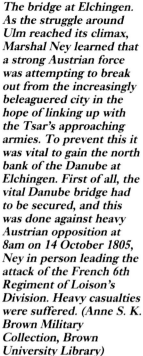

The bridge at Elchingen. As the struggle around Ulm reached its climax, Marshal Ney learned that a strong Austrian force was attempting to break out from the increasingly beleaguered city in the hope of linking up with the Tsar's approaching armies. To prevent this it was vital to gain the north bank of the Danube at Elchingen. First of all, the vital Danube bridge had to be secured, and this was done against heavy Austrian opposition at 8am on 14 October 1805, Ney in person leading the attack of the French 6th Regiment of Loison's Division. Heavy casualties were suffered. (Anne S. K. Brown Military Collection, Brown University Library)

The Abbey at Elchingen. From Elchingen bridge the French stormed uphill to challenge the Austrian main force arriving from the west under Generals Werneck and Riesch. A fierce fight for control of Ober-Elchingen raged all morning through the streets of the small town and particularly around the large abbey church and its walled surrounds. By midday on the 14th, the French were masters of the area and the Austrians in full retreat for Ulm. Napoleon commended Ney on this success. (Anne S. K. Brown Military Collection, Brown University Library)

attacks into the Black Forest east of the Rhine to distract Mack's attention for what was happening elsewhere.

The *Grande Armée* comprised seven corps besides Murat's cavalry and the Bavarian army (which would be incorporated in due course). I Corps, some 17,000 men commanded by Bernadotte, consisted of the French occupation forces in Hanover; II Corps, 15,000 French and 5,000 Dutch troops drawn from Holland, advanced under Marmont to Mainz; III Corps, 26,000 strong, left Ambleteuse for Mannheim under command of Davout. A little further south moved Soult at the head of IV Corps, made up of 40,000 men from the camp of Boulogne, with Ney's 24,000 men of VI Corps on his right from the same Channel area, both corps heading for the right bank of the Rhine opposite Karlsruhe, where Ney temporarily added a division of Badeners to his command. Towards Strasbourg rode Murat's 22,000 cavalry, followed by the 7,000 members of the Imperial Guard under Bessières and Lannes' V Corps (18,000 strong). Some way to the rear moved Augereau's VII Corps (14,000 men from the vicinity of Brest) charged with protecting the army's lines of communication. Plans were also in hand to create a reserve corps of Bavarians, Badeners and Württembergers (eventually 26,000 strong) to be entrusted with similar duties. A total of 396 guns and their crews moved with the army, but wagon convoys were severely restricted in size on the Emperor's orders.

The strategic movement was concealed for as long as possible. Writing to Bernadotte on 5 September, Napoleon ordered him to act as follows: 'You will announce everywhere that you are returning to France because you are being relieved by Dutch troops. Let them believe what they like – but it is none the less necessary not to deviate from this conversational theme.' Three weeks later the meeting of I and II Corps at Würzburg (29 September) was declared to be for the purpose of holding joint manoeuvres, although by that date the campaign had opened.

By the 20th, Murat's cavalry had reached Strasbourg, and by the 24th all major formations (save only Augereau's) were ready on the west bank of the Rhine. Travelling from Paris, Napoleon was at Nancy on the 25th, aware that the corps had begun to cross the river the night before. The French advanced at first through fine autumnal weather, averaging about 30 kilometres a day, each corps following its separate route as prescribed, but all steadily converging as planned on the River Danube. The die was irrevocably cast.

Strategic Triumph – the Manoeuvre of Ulm

Just eleven days after crossing the Rhine, the first French troops were passing over the Danube. It was only on the 30th that a bewildered General Mack came to realize that he was about to be attacked from the rear, and not through the Black Forest as anticipated. Concentrating his Austrians just to the east of Ulm, for a time Mack tried to persuade himself that rumours of a British landing at Boulogne were causing his opponents to retreat towards the French frontier. However, there was no disguising the fact that there was no sign of Kutusov's Russians. Dazed by the rapidity and unconventional nature of the events that were unfolding the Austrian commanders did virtually nothing – and so sealed their fate.

So far the French advance had gone remarkably well, even if Bernadotte had violated the neutrality of Prussian Ansbach en route for the Danube, a deed that infuriated Frederick William III at Berlin. After crossing the great river well to the east of Ulm on 7 October at Münster, Dönauwörth, Neuburg and Ingolstädt, the French set about encompassing Mack's doom as the corps of the *Grande Armée* fanned out from the south bank. The first action was fought at Wertingen on the 8th, the Austrians having the worst of the encounter. Sending I and III Corps east with the Bavarian troops to occupy the line of the River Isar, ready to ward off any Russian intervention, and IV Corps south to Augsburg and Landsberg to guard against the forces of Archduke John attempting to move north, Napoleon turned west with II, V and VI Corps, the Imperial Guard and the cavalry, expecting to fight Mack and the Archduke Ferdinand near the River Iller. In this the Emperor for once miscalculated – as the Austrians eventually made a series of half-hearted attempts to break out along the north bank, and an error by Murat led to Dupont's division of Ney's VI Corps finding itself in dangerous isolation fighting a large Austrian force at Haslach on 11 October; but fine fighting by the 6,000 troops trounced their opponents and induced Mack to draw back closer to Ulm. Three days later Ney forced a river crossing to the north bank at Elchingen, defeated Reisch, and, rejoining Dupont, moved towards Ulm. Far to the south the French took possession of Memmingen.

A serious row in Austrian headquarters resulted in Ferdinand taking the cavalry away to the north-east, but for Mack and the remainder of his army there was no escape as the French net tightened around the city. Murat's cavalry were

The French March to Ulm

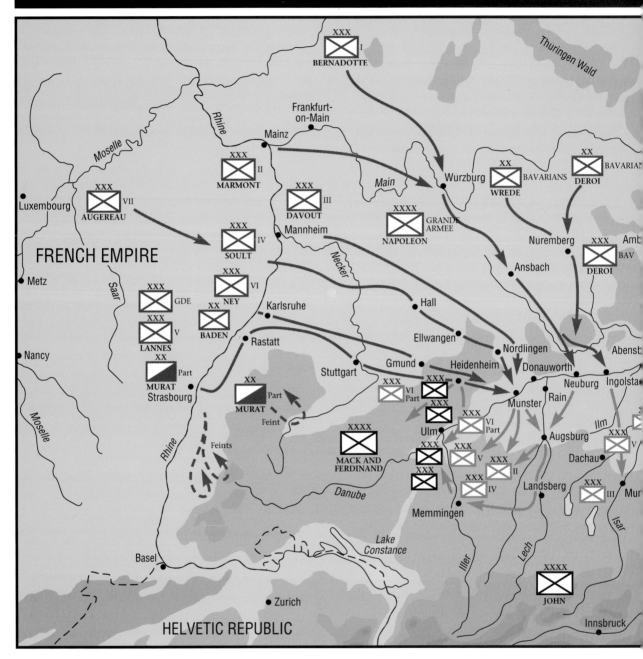

soon in hot pursuit of the Archduke, while VI Corps, supported by the Guard, seized the Michelsberg Heights overlooking Ulm on the 15th, following a second action at Haslach, as Napoleon moved Lannes' V Corps north over Elchingen bridge, and Soult moved in upon Ulm from the south-west. Mack, still hoping for Kutusov's arrival from the east, was now practically surrounded.

Hoping to win time for Russian aid to materialize, he opened negotiations with the French on the 16th. Next day Mack agreed that he would surrender on the 25th unless help had reached him. But the French negotiators produced strong evidence that Kutusov was still far distant, and the doomed Mack eventually capitulated on the 20th, five days early. Some 27,000 Austrian troops filed

he Approach to Austerlitz

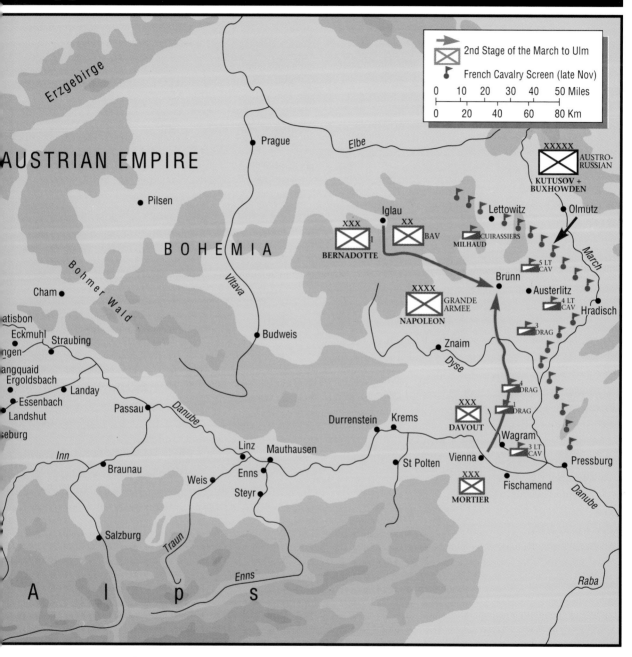

out to lay down their arms as their commander introduced himself to the conqueror as 'the unfortunate General Mack'. Away to the north-east Murat forced successive detachments of Austrian cavalry and infantry of Ferdinand and General Werneck to surrender. Mack's army was no more.

For the loss of some 2,000 casualties, in two weeks the *Grande Armée* had accounted for 4,000 Austrians and taken almost 60,000 prisoners of war with 80 colours and 200 cannon – all without recourse to a major battle. As his exhausted but ecstatic infantry declared, 'the Emperor has invented a new way of making war: he makes it more with our legs than with our arms!'

It had been an amazing achievement – but there were still some 300,000 Allies to be accounted for.

Furthermore, on 21 October – the same day that Mack's army marched out of Ulm, far away to the south-west off Cape Trafalgar Vice-Admiral Lord Nelson had won a massive victory over Vice-Admiral Villeneuve's Franco-Spanish fleet as it left Cadiz, albeit at the cost of his own life. Henceforth the Royal Navy could claim mastery of the seas.

The Pursuit of the Russians

As soon as General Kutusov learnt of the fate that had befallen General Mack, he at once ordered a retreat over the River Inn. Napoleon launched his army in pursuit on the 26th, after regrouping his forces around Munich and Landshut. The Russian commander had 36,000 Russians and 22,000 Austrians under command, and his sole thought was to pass over the Danube to the north bank and retire in the direction of Buxhöwden's approaching Russian army, 30,000 strong. March as they might, however, the French could never quite catch the elusive Kutusov. On the 28th the French were over the Inn, but, although there were a number of fierce skirmishes with Russian and Austrian rearguards at successive river-lines, the wily commander kept always one move ahead of the French pursuit, which was in three columns. Passing the River Enns, the Emperor created a provisional corps by taking a division from each of II, V and VI Corps, and awarded its command to Marshal Mortier with orders to advance along the Danube's northern bank. As these formations were widely dispersed, with immediate effect Mortier found himself in command of only Gazan's Division of V Corps. On other sectors, Ney had repulsed Archduke John near Innsbruck; meanwhile in North Italy, Massena and Archduke Charles had fought an indecisive battle at Caldiero near Verona on 29 and 30 October – but the Austrians withdrew behind the River Tagliamento to cover Archduke John's withdrawal from the Tyrol.

By 9 November Kutusov had successfully withdrawn over the Danube near Krems – and received 10,000 reinforcements. Two days later he fell upon the isolated Mortier at Durrenstein (or Dürnstein) with 15,000 men, but by late on the 11th Gazan had been joined by Dupont, and between them they had successfully fought off the

attack. Napoleon was furious at his oversight concerning Mortier, and vented his wrath upon Murat, who had ridden into Vienna on the 12th, followed by Lannes and Soult. Murat redeemed himself by seizing a bridge over the Danube in the city by means of a piece of consummate bluff. Accompanied by Lannes, he boldly walked across in full view of the Austrians, declaring that an armistice had been concluded, and fooled the bridge's defenders until a force of grenadiers arrived in their midst. Napoleon, learning that Kutusov was retiring north towards Znaim, ordered Bernadotte over the Danube at Molk, while the cavalry, V and IV Corps were to cross over the Vienna bridge, with Davout moving up to occupy the Austrian capital behind them. The Emperor still hoped to catch Kutusov before he met Buxhöwden. On the 15th, Napoleon was himself in Vienna.

Unfortunately for the French, the Russian rearguard commander, General Bagration, fooled Murat in his turn with talk of a spurious armistice at Hollabrünn on 15 November. 'I am lost for words with which to express my displeasure,' wrote Napoleon,' … you have thrown away the advantages of the entire campaign.' Murat at once broke the armistice and attacked Bagration, only to find that his opponent had withdrawn after a hard day's fighting around the bridge at Schöngraben – and had thus eluded him. Even worse news was to follow, for on 20 November Kutusov at last joined Büxhowden to form a joint army of some 86,000 men. More reassuring was news found in a captured Austrian dispatch which revealed that Archduke Charles, slowly retiring before a lackadaisical Massena, was unlikely to reach Leoben (occupied by Marmont's II Corps) before the 24th; meanwhile, in the Tyrol, Ney and the Bavarians were hot on the heels of the retreating Archduke John and his scattered components. Reassured about his distant southern flank for the time being, Napoleon decided to press on northwards after the Russians.

On the 17th Napoleon was at Znaim, aware that all his hopes of catching Kutusov on his own were unlikely to be fulfilled. Furthermore, he was only too aware that his army had almost reached the limit of its strength and desperately needed a period

The meeting of Napoleon and Mack, after Boutigny. In a famous scene, the Austrian General surrenders to Napoleon at Ulm in October 1805. The collapse of Austrian resistance on the Danube was the first great French success in the campaign of 1805. (Author's Collection)

The combat of Amstetten, by Chavane after Siméon Fort. On 5 November, Prince Murat, leading the French advance eastwards south of the Danube at the head of several regiments of light cavalry, unexpectedly encountered a strong Russian rearguard as his horsemen emerged from the snow-girt forest of Amstetten. A stiff engagement developed, ended by darkness. Both sides claimed success. (Anne S. K. Brown Military Collection, Brown University Library)

The action of Dürnstein by Larbalestion after Siméon Fort. After successfully completing their crossing of the Danube to the north bank, on 11 December the Russians attacked the only French formation on their side of the river – namely Marshal Mortier's extemporized VIII Corps of 5,500 men encamped around Dürnstein. The heroic struggle that ensued is here viewed from south of the Danube. (Anne S. K. Brown Military Collection, Brown University Library)

French light infantry musicians; colour print by J. Onfroy de Bréville, after Job. (Philip J. Haythornthwaite)

to rest and reorganize. There were also worrying signs that Prussia might be on the point of entering the war – which would mean an accession of another 200,000 men to the Third Coalition. By this time, after all the many detachments the campaign had required to date, Napoleon had barely 53,000 soldiers under direct command, and so on 23 November he called a halt at Brünn. Bernadotte and his I Corps were ordered, together with Wrede's Bavarians, to occupy Iglau to the north-west of Brünn, and there to keep a weather eye open for the Archduke Ferdinand (who had avoided capture after the Ulm fiasco) believed to be marching from Prague with 18,000 men, and also for any indications of Prussian hostile intentions. But Napoleon realized his problems in his present position all too well. Given time, Archdukes Charles and John might be able to arrive from the south while Napoleon was not at present even

strong enough to fight the Russo-Austrian army massing around Olmütz, some 30 miles north-east of Brünn, where it had been joined by both Tsar Alexander and the Emperor of Austria. All in all, the omens did not look propitious.

Lead-up to the Battle of Austerlitz

The weather had turned bitterly cold, which added to the discomfiture of Murat's, Lannes' and Soult's ragged and hungry formations as they gathered near Brünn, at the extreme limit of the *Grande Armée's* advance, and huddled over the warmth of their camp fires. The men grumbled, their officers conjectured. News of Trafalgar, or a renewed financial crisis in Paris, or a reappearance of Bourbon sympathizers in France, were not designed to cheer men who were facing superior numbers of foes and were at least 700 miles from their homeland's frontiers. The situation appeared potentially disastrous.

Napoleon, however, was always at his best in a crisis. He at once determined to lure the Allies into a precipitate attack against a position and at a time of his own choosing. This would require much guile and careful preparation – and the Emperor bent all his mental energies to the challenge. On 21 November he conducted a reconnaissance accompanied by his staff. As de Ségur wrote: 'On going back from Wischau he stopped on the highway about two leagues and a half from Brünn, near the Santon – a small mound by the side of the road, a kind of abruptly truncated cone – and gave orders that the foot of it should be excavated on the enemy's side so as to increase its escarpment. Then, turning off towards the south, he entered a high plain contained between two embanked streams running from the north to the south-west. The Emperor slowly and silently went over this newly discovered ground, stopping several times on its most elevated points, looking principally towards Pratzen [to the east]. He carefully examined all its characteristics and during this survey turned towards us, saying: "Gentlemen, examine this ground carefully. It is going to be a battlefield: you will have a part to play upon it." This plain was indeed to be within a few days the field of the battle of Austerlitz.'

But how to lure the foe to attack? Napoleon soon devised a plan. Murat, Lannes and Soult were ordered to advance towards Wischau and Olmütz to draw the enemy's attention and occupy the town of Austerlitz and the intervening Pratzen Heights, pushing a cavalry brigade even farther forward. By showing the 85,000-strong enemy a force of about 53,000 men he felt sure they would be tempted to attack. Once he was confident that the enemy were taking the proffered bait, Napoleon intended to call up by forced marches both Bernadotte's I Corps from Iglau and Davout's III Corps from Vienna, bringing his strength up to some 75,000 men for the battle – reducing the numerical odds against him to more manageable proportions.

By the 25th the preliminary moves had been completed. How would the foe react? At Olmütz the Allies hesitated – there being considerable friction between the Russian and Austrian senior officers forming the council of war. By the 24th, they had decided on a counter-offensive. Only Kutusov and the Austrian Emperor advocated caution, while the Tsar listened to his fire-eating aides and to such Austrian generals as Weyrother, Kollowrath and Kienmayer, who were burning to avenge the humiliation of Ulm. Next day, an Austrian delegation was sent under flag of truce to Napoleon to discuss the possibility of an armistice – and also to take a close look at the condition of the Frency army. The Emperor was the personification of charm and gratitude, but sent the delegation off to Vienna to negotiate with Talleyrand, the Foreign Minister. Napoleon then sent off General Savary, his keen-witted chief of intelligence, to convey his desire for an armistice to the Tsar and the Austrian Emperor – and also to make an assessment of Allied intentions and capabilities.

On the 28th, Napoleon was interviewing the Prussian Foreign Minister, Haugwitz, whose master was making a great play to act as international mediator, when news arrived that Bagration had driven Murat's cavalry out of Wischau (as Napoleon had intended) and was engaging Soult's outposts. Referring Haugwitz to Talleyrand in Vienna, Napoleon at once called for his horse and rode to the outpost line. There he met the returning Savary, who presented the Tsar's reply, insultingly addressed to 'the Head of the

Officer, élite company of the French 5th Hussars of Kellermann's Division, showing the typical winter campaign uniform with headdress ornaments removed and the pelisse worn as a jacket. Colour print after Edouard Détaille. (Philip J. Haythornthwaite)

French government'. This document – as expected – made impossibly high demands in terms of concessions and cessions of territory, but more to the point were Savary's personal impressions. He reported that the Allied counsels were still divided, the Emperor Francis and Kutusov advising circumspection but the hot-heads demanding an all-out attack. They were representing Napoleon's apparent willingness to negotiate as a sure sign of weakness and pointing out that the exhaustion of local foodstuffs made a move imperative. Moreover, these advisers undoubtedly had the ear of Alexander. Savary further reported that when he had left Olmütz there were clear signs of large-scale troop movements to the west towards Brünn.

Napoleon at once dispatched urgent messages to Iglau and Vienna to call Bernadotte and Davout to Brünn forthwith and setting up a screen of cavalry to disguise these critical moves from Austrian or Russian patrols. News from the distant theatres was acceptable. Although he could not know it, the Archdukes Charles and John had joined at Marburg on the 26th of the month to make a joint army of 80,000 men, but Massena (35,000) had been sent fresh orders on the 22nd demanding a pursuit 'without respite'. Between the Archdukes and the road towards Vienna from Styria stood Marmont with the 15,000 men of II Corps around Leoben and Graz. He was ordered to prepare to march closer to Vienna if need arose. Saint Cyr with 15,000 men was besieging 12,000 Austrians locked in Venice. Most important of all, there was still no clear sign of a Prussian decision in favour of war, although it was known that the Tsar's ambassadors were pressing the point in Berlin. In overall terms, therefore, the scene was set for a major confrontation of arms in frost-bound Moravia.

Now that the Allies had snapped up the bait and were duly hooked it was necessary to play them in the right direction. Napoleon accordingly determined to foster still further the illusion of French weakness. Savary was sent back to Allied headquarters with a request from Napoleon for a personal interview – and thus given a second chance to observe the state of the enemy army. Alexander refused the request, but sent his most arrogant aide-de-camp, Count Dolgorouki, to visit the French Emperor. Napoleon put on a show of anxious courtesy, even riding to the outpost line to meet the envoy. Dolgorouki – 'a youthful trumpeter of England' Napoleon would later term him in his Bulletin – then treated his distinguished interlocutor to a lecture on European politics (which impudence the Emperor accepted with a grave expression), before returning to the Tsar 'full of the notion that the French army was on the eve of its doom'. Next, an astounded Soult was sent orders to abandon both the town of Austerlitz and the critical terrain of the Pratzen Heights with every appearance of indecent haste. It was done, and the foe was reported to be moving south-westwards hesitantly and in considerable confusion in the direction of the vacated area, just as Napoleon intended they should. By surrendering such

important ground to the Allies, Napoleon appeared to be uncovering his right flank and beyond it the high road running south to Vienna – in other words his lines of communication and possible retreat. For it was important that the enemy should mount a major outflanking move against the French right as this manoeuvre would in all likelihood cause them to uncover their own centre and line of retreat beyond it. In fact this did not represent as big a risk to the French as might at first appear, for Napoleon now possessed a second line of retreat running due west from Brünn towards Iglau, whereas the Allies enjoyed no such advantage.

On 30 November the last French cavalry detachments abandoned Wishau with every sign of disorder, even panic, and the Allies ponderously moved forward towards Austerlitz and the Pratzen. 'It was no longer merely a question of fighting the French army, but of turning its flank and overwhelming it.' So matters stood on 1 December. That day Bernadotte's I Corps arrived unostentatiously from Iglau (leaving Wrede's Bavarians there to guard the French left rear) to be halted in a valley behind the Zurlan Height, which was to form Napoleon's command post. Although few present could guess it, one of the most masterly of Napoleon's stratagems was about to deliver the soldiers of Holy Russia and Imperial Austria into his hands.

THE OPPOSING COMMANDERS

The Emperor Napoleon I

In 1805, Napoleon was 35 years of age. Since 1796 – when he first emerged as a great military commander – his name had become synonymous with that of France, his adopted country. Since 1799 his meteoric political career had matched his military rise, culminating in his crowning in December 1804 as Emperor.

As a soldier, Napoleon's talents were truly impressive. Much of his skill was opportunistic, but as the 'master of the alternate plan' he could adjust his strategic and grand tactical (or operational) plans to circumstances, as both the switch from the River Iller to an attack upon Ulm, and his moulding of the events leading up to, and as we shall see during, the battle of Austerlitz illustrate. Risks he certainly accepted, but they were never rashly inspired. His strategic skills were daunting, as the great wheel through Germany from the Rhine to the Danube, one of the greatest military movements in history, demonstrated. Perhaps he paid less attention to logistics than was desirable, but the gamble of the troops being able to 'live off the countryside' to a marked degree was justifiable in central Europe or Italy (although by 2 December his men were decidedly hungry in frost-bound Moravia), but in later years this aspect of his science of war would lead to immense difficulties in Spain and then western Russia. But it was at the joint-levels of leadership and man-management that he excelled. His relationship with his officers and men was often stormy, but his reputation as a victorious, hard-fighting commander was already well developed by 1805, and his pyschological dominance over his chosen instrument – *la Grande Armée* – was complete. So was his intellectual dominance over his enemies, however much they chose to delude themselves that they had his measure in the last days of November. Napoleon was often ruthless, self-centred, tactless and arrogant, but he lent a dynamism to the conduct of war that had not been seen since Alexander the Great. The events of 2 December 1805 were about to demonstrate once again his mastery of 'the bloody solution of the crisis', to cite Clausewitz. It is only to be regretted that the path ahead of him would see a remorseless decade of destructive war after destructive war, as this circumstance obviously dominated his life, and that of Europe, and put a discount on his equally impressive creative talents. He never proved capable of achieving a lasting peace, due to his demanding terms and ill-concealed scorn for his outclassed and humbled opponents. And yet he himself had stated that 'war, like government, is a matter of tact'. There was indeed one fundamental weakness in his overpowering intellect, which was spotted in the latter years of the Empire by one of his most perceptive ministers. 'It is an amazing fact,' wrote Count Nicolas Mollien, 'that although his common sense amounted to genius, somehow he never knew when the possible left off.' Napoleon became the personification of the warlord. Nevertheless, he was undoubtedly one of history's greatest men, and the events of 1805 (backed by those of 1806 against Prussia) once and for all showed him to be the greatest soldier since the dawn of the age of gunpowder. As Sièyes percipiently remarked during the Consulate: '*Il fait tout; il sait tout; il peut tout.*' ('He does everything; he knows everything; he can do anything.')

The Emperor Napoleon: a bronze by R. Colombo. In August 1805, Napoleon celebrated his 36th birthday. Already a soldier and statesman of international renown, he had been Emperor since 2 December the previous year. Before the year of 1805 was out he would have added fresh laurels to his reputation and proved the worth of his creation, la Grande Armée. (Ben Weider Collection)

Napoleon's Opponents at Austerlitz

One of the names given to the climacteric struggle about to begin is 'the Battle of the Three Emperors'. One major reason for the decisive outcome of the day's fighting of 2 December 1805 was the hydra-headed Allied senior command system (one cannot say 'supreme', as no-one wielded the type of authority enjoyed by Napoleon). The presence on the field of two emperors and one supposed commander-in-chief proved a fatal complication for the Allies.

Tsar Alexander I of the House of Romanov was a tall, handsome man of 27 years. On 24 March 1801 he had succeeded to the thone of 'All the Russias' on the demise of his hated father, the mad Tsar Paul, as a result of a palace intrigue at St Petersburg in which the son was almost certainly implicated. Both vain and highly impressionable, Alexander was at first almost mesmerized by Napoleon's reputation, but for reasons already described he had joined the Third Coalition against France. A ruler of considerable ability, he was nobody's idea of a great or even a competent soldier – except, tragically, in his own estimation. He surrounded himself with a *jeunesse dorée* of wealthy young noblemen, who flattered their master to the extent that he came to believe himself infallible, and who sneered at the cautious counsels of older and wiser men. In later years of his reign, Alexander became a religious mystic and withdrew himself from the day-to-day management of his vast empire of some 44 million souls. But in 1805 he was the personification of charm and grace – and, less fortunately, of an asinine stubborness. Some regarded him as tending towards effeminacy, and others have queried the ultimate stability of his personality. Certainly he was no intellectual match for Napoleon, as the Conference of Tilsit would demonstrate in 1807. Although personally courageous, neither was he a soldier, and only the accident of his birth brought him to a position where he could meddle and interfere with the conduct of a major battle – and yet at the same time inspire an unquestioning obedience to his whims among his fellow-Russians, however disastrous they would prove. Alexander was the epitome of the early 19th century despot.

Tsar Alexander I, by Baron Gérard. Alexander succeeded his father, 'mad Tsar Paul I', in 1801. His fascination for Napoleon diminished after the execution of the Duke d'Enghien in 1804, and he took Russia into the Third Coalition against France. Accompanying his army into the field, he repeatedly listened to the hotheads on his staff and overruled the sage counsels of the nominal commander-in-chief, Kutusov: this proved a major factor in the catastrophe that befell Russian and Austrian arms at Austerlitz. (Author's collection)

The Emperor Francis II. Francis II (1768–1835) succeeded Leopold II in 1792 as ruler of the Holy Roman Empire and was at Austerlitz in this capacity in December 1805. Shortly after the battle he met Napoleon to agree an armistice, which eventually led to the Peace of Pressburg. After Napoleon abolished the Holy Roman Empire (which Voltaire had described as 'neither holy, nor Roman, least of all an empire'), Francis changed his title to become Francis I of Austria. It is by this title that he is most commonly known. (Anne S. K. Brown Military Collection, Brown University)

Mikhail Hilarionovich Golenischev-Kutusov. Kutusov (1745–1813) was one of the ablest of Tsar Alexander's generals, eventually attaining the title of Prince and the rank of field marshal. After many successes against the Turks, in 1805 he was given command of the main Russian army for the German campaign. Arriving too late to succour the Austrian General Mack at Ulm, he conducted a model withdrawal to Olmütz, where he linked with Buxhöwden's army. His doubts about the wisdom of fighting Napoleon at Austerlitz were overruled by the Tsar but proved all too well founded. His greatest achievements lay ahead in 1812. (Author's collection)

The Emperor Francis II of the House of Habsburg was a very different man from his fellow-ruler. Aged 38 in December 1805, he looked far more than ten year's older than the Tsar. He had succeeded Leopold II in 1792 as Holy Roman Emperor (or Emperor of Germany), and his reign had so far seen little but disaster. This had prematurely aged him. He had been forced to cede large areas of territory at the close of the wars of the First and Second Coalitions. By the Peace of Campo Formio (1797) he had given up the Austrian Netherlands (today Belgium) to France, abandoned Lombardy in North Italy, and had been forced to recognise the Ligurian and Cisalpine Republics, receiving only Dalmatia, the Frioul near Trieste, and Venetian territory to the east of the Adige in a decidedly unfair exchange. He had also been forced to accept by secret treaty French claims to all territory up to the Rhine, besides French occupation of the strategically important Mediterranean Ionian Isles and Corfu. After Marengo and Hohenlinden, Austria had fared little better. By the Peace of Lunéville (February 1801), Francis had been compelled to confirm the earlier cessions insofar as they involved North Italian, Rhenish and Swiss affairs, and in return had secured some form of compensation for disinherited German princes in the Rhine valley, the restoration of the Neapolitan Bourbons to their Kingdom of Naples, and the award of Tuscany to the Duke of Parma in return for his own principality now incorporated in the Cisalpine Republic. Near bankruptcy was threatening the Empire. Now, to cap it all, the war of 1805 had got off to a disastrous start at Ulm, and his capital of Vienna and palace of Schönbrunn, together with almost half of the Austrian homeland, were all occupied by the French. Francis had therefore good reason for glum depression as he advocated caution in the Allied discussions at Olmütz. With scant prestige, however, he was accorded only formal attention by the Russian favourites, and even his own generals – thirsting for revenge for the humiliations recently heaped upon their army – backed the strident

General Weyrother, 'a veteran of the Viennese offices', as he unfolded the grandiose plan of battle at 1am on 1 December.

Only one Russian general seemed to pay due heed to the Austrian Emperor's view of the need for great caution – namely Kutusov, the *de facto* overall commander-in-chief, whose authority was in fact totally undermined by his royal master's presence. Aged 60, the son of a military engineer, Kutusov's service had begun in the artillery of Catherine the Great. From the gunners he had transferred to the new *jaeger* formations and had rapidly risen to command that corps. Between 1764 and 1769 he had campaigned with growing distinction in Poland and the Ukraine, and then from 1770 to 1774 in the Crimea against the Turks, during which period he had lost an eye in action. This wound was followed by the receipt of a shot in the head at the siege of Ochakov in 1788, but he recovered from this in time to play a distinguished role in the operations that cleared the Turks from the important towns of Odessa, Benda and Ismail.

Sent as ambassador to Constantinople, he was later made governor of the new Russian province of Finland, from which post he was transferred in 1805 to the command of the main Russian army with orders to make common cause with Austria. A cunning and experienced commander, with not a little Tartar blood in his lineage, he had fought an effective withdrawal from the River Inn to Olmütz, at the price of seeing the French occupy Vienna. Regarded as a dotard by the bright sprigs around the Tsar, he found the presence of two Emperors at his headquarters an impossible complication – and proved powerless to withstand the Tsar's demands for immediate action – although Kutusov considered it both premature and perilous. At Weyrother's conference he was seen to doze off after a very few minutes, and 'fell into a sound nap before our departure', as General Langeron noted. There is no doubt, however, that Kutusov was a soldier of distinction and experience, with the power to inspire a high level of response from the common soldiers of Muscovy. He was invariably courteous, exceedingly shrewd and knowledgeable, as even his many critics admitted. However, he also had his faults. He was fond of both the bottle and of sporting with young women a third his own age. But

he was a colourful figure, whose full greatness would only emerge seven years later – at and after the great battle of Borodino.

As de Ségur would record of this stalwart soldier in 1812, Kutusov's 'valour was incontestable, but he was charged with regulating its vehemence according to his private interest; for he calculated everything. His genius was slow, vindictive, and above all crafty – the true Tartar character! – knowing the art of preparing a fawning, supple and patient policy.' Today, Kutusov is still regarded with awe and approval in the USSR, thanks to writing conducted by the former Lieutenant-General Pavel Zhilin, the late head of the Military History Institute of the Soviet Union. Comparing his hero to Napoleon, Zhilin wrote as follows in 1978: 'If M. I. Kutusov's military legacy was depreciated or simply ignored in Russian official historiography of the 19th century, then Napoleonic military art was exalted in excess. Its active propagandist was General Jomini, of Swiss origin. . . . Enthusiasm for Napoleon's military art . . . brought with it a devaluing of . . . the legacy of . . . Kutusov.' But at Austerlitz he was to prove no match for Napoleon.

THE OPPOSING ARMIES

La Grande Armée d'Allemagne

Napoleon's army of 1805 was a finely-tempered weapon upon which a great deal of careful thought and painstaking endeavour had been applied in organizational and training terms during the years following the joint-peaces of Lunéville (1801) and Amiens (1802), which had brought the War of the Second Coalition to a close – and for a brief spell brought France and Europe the blessings of peace. The *Grande Armée d'Allemagne* reflected all of Napoleon's experience since 1796, and its showing at Ulm and, above all, Austerlitz was to prove it to be the finest in service.

From 1800 the French army was made up of a number of *corps d'armée* (army corps), which were the key operational units. Each corps was an all-arm formation with its own staff, commanded by a marshal or senior general. It comprised varying numbers of infantry divisions, a light cavalry brigade or division, and an artillery detachment under corps command (between six and a dozen, or occasionally more, 12pdrs, nicknamed 'the Emperor's beautiful daughters'). It also contained engineer (*le génie*) and bridging (*pontonier*) detachments), the latter in fact being part of the artillery service, besides its own supply and medical units. The size of a corps varied enormously, depending upon Napoleon's view of its intended role and the capacity of its commander. The composition was fluid and its organization highly flexible, permitting changes to be implemented in mid-campaign (as in the case of the creation of a new VIII Corps under Marshal Mortier during the

French infantrymen. In 1805 many French infantrymen still wore the bicorn hat rather than the shako. The pack was made of animal skin, with the hair outwards, to protect its contents from dampness. (Anne S. K. Brown Military Collection, Brown University)

A French light cavalry officer. French light cavalry comprised mainly hussars and chasseurs. The print depicts a French officer of chasseurs-à-cheval wearing the typical fur busby and cloak, and armed with a curved sabre and pair of pistols. (Anne S. K. Brown Military Collection, Brown University)

second phase of the campaign of 1805, to the utter confusion of Austrian military intelligence). In this year the largest corps was the 40,000 men of Marshal Soult, who was to earn the title of 'the foremost manoeuverer in Europe' from the Emperor. The smallest were Augereau's VII Corps (14,000) and Mortier's extemporized VIII Corps (a nominal 15,000 made up of divisions taken from

French Chasseur à Pied of the Imperial Guard; colour print by Martinet.

(Philip J. Haythornthwaite)

Marmont, Lannes and Ney). A corps was, in effect, a miniature army, capable of marching and subsisting on its own and of fighting or holding down several times its own number until assistance could arrive. It was one of Napoleon's golden rules that a corps should be within supporting range of at least one other major formation (i.e., a day's march of up to 22 miles).

An infantry division consisted of up to 16,000 men in theory, although rarely in practice, comprising two (occasionally more) brigades of two regiments apiece, renamed from the *demi-brigades* of the Revolutionary Wars, and a battery of six guns, habitually four 8pdrs and two 6in howitzers, the whole force commanded by a general aided by a small staff. A regiment had three battalions of up to 1,200 men apiece and included a band, a medical detachment and a small wagon section for the regimental baggage and munitions. Some regiments also controlled a *compagnie* of four 4pdr (sometimes 6 pdr) cannon and two howitzers. A regiment was often a colonel's command.

A battalion – the basic tactical unit – was commanded by a major, and comprised nine companies, including one of *voltigeurs* (literally 'leapers'), or light infantry, who in action formed a skirmishing screen ahead of the main body and one grenadier company of élite troops. In addition to regiments of line infantry, there were complete units of *tirailleurs*, or light infantry, comprising a *carabinier* company (the equivalent of line grenadiers), one of *voltigeurs* and a larger number of companies of *chasseurs à pied*. All other ranks were armed with the Charleville pattern '1777' smoothbore 0.70in flintlock musket, firing balls weighing 4/5ths of an ounce, and carried 50 cartridges containing powder and ball in a *giberne*, or cartridge-box, besides a bayonet and short sword. The musket had a range of over 250 yards but was not very accurate at over 100 yards. A pack, cooking pot and blanket roll completed a soldier's campaign equipment.

Napoleon also created a Cavalry Reserve under Prince Murat, his brother-in-law and the foremost

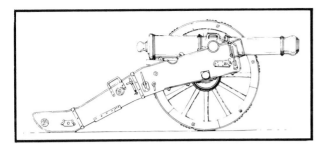

French cannon. 'It is with guns that war is made,' stated Napoleon, himself a gunner in his youth. The French artillery, thanks to the reforms of Count de Gribeauval (1715–89), was the best in Europe. Lighter barrels, improved casting methods, better-designed trails, careful training – all contributed to this achievement. Most important of all, however, was his 'System's' classification of guns into just four calibres or types: the 12pdr, the 8pdr, the 4pdr (later replaced by the 6pdr) and the 6in howitzer. The principle of adding two howitzers to every 'company' (battery) was also important. Under Napoleon, the heaviest cannon were placed in the Artillery Reserve (with lighter horse and 'flying' artillery batteries) and at Army Corps level, while 8pdrs served with divisions and the light guns at regimental level. (Anne S. K. Brown Military Collection, Brown University)

French Sergeant-Major with 'Eagle' of the 4ème Ligne. Illustration by Bryan Fosten.

beau sabreur of the Europe of his day. This formation contained divisions of 'heavy' cuirassiers (wearing helmets with horse-hair plumes, back- and breast-plates, and armed with long straight swords, carbines, and a pair of pistols); more of dragoons (who carried flintlock muskets as well as swords and were in theory capable of dismounted as well as mounted action); and yet more divisions of light cavalry, including hussars and chasseurs equipped with pistols and curved slashing sabres, whose primary tasks were scouting, reconnaissance and pursuit. He also developed what would become an Artillery Reserve of 12pdrs and highly mobile horse artillery equipped with 6pdr guns. Most cannon fired either solid shot or canister for short-range anti-personnel work, but howitzers fired exploding shells lit by a fuse. Artillery ranges varied between 1,800 yards for a 12pdr to 1,500 yards for a piece of 8, and 1,200 for a 4pdr. Effective ranges were more in the order of 900, 800 and 600 yards respectively, although use of ricochet fire could increase ranges by half or more for solid shot under the right conditions.

LA GRANDE ARMEE

Commander-in-Chief: the Emperor Napoleon
Chief of Staff: Marshal Louis Alexandre Berthier

The Imperial Guard Marshal Jean Baptiste Bessières
INFANTRY OF THE GUARD:
1st and 2nd Battalions *Grenadiers à Pied* (foot grenadiers)
1st and 2nd Battalions *Chasseurs à Pied* (light infantry)
The Grenadiers of the Royal Italian Guard
CAVALRY OF THE GUARD:
Grenadiers à Cheval (horse grenadiers)
Chasseurs à Cheval (light cavalry)
Les Mamelukes (brigaded with the *Chasseurs à Cheval*
Gendarmerie d'Elite
ARTILLERY OF THE GUARD:
Light Artillery of the Guard
Artillery Train of the Guard
Strength at Austerlitz: 5,500 men and 24 guns.

I Corps Marshal Jean Baptiste Bernadotte
ADVANCE GUARD: *27ème Régiment d'Infanterie Légère* (light infantry)
1ST DIVISION: General of Division Olivier Rivaud de la Raffinière
8ème Régiment d'Infanterie de Ligne (line infantry)
45ème Régiment d'Infanterie de Ligne
54ème Régiment d'Infanterie de Ligne
2ND DIVISION: General of Division Jean Baptiste Drouet
94ème Régiment d'Infanterie de Ligne
95ème Régiment d'Infanterie de Ligne
LIGHT CAVALRY DIVISION: General François Etienne Kellermann
(Attached to Murat's Cavalry Reserve on 2 December; see below)
Strength at Austerlitz (infantry and artillery): 13,000 men and 24 guns.

III Corps Marshal Louis Nicolas Davout
2ND DIVISION: General of Division Louis Friant
15ème Régiment d'Infanterie Légère
33ème Régiment d'Infanterie de Ligne
48ème Régiment d'Infanterie de Ligne
108ème Régiment d'Infanterie de Ligne

111ème Régiment d'Infanterie de Ligne
4TH DRAGOON DIVISION: General François Antoine Louis Bourcier
15ème Régiment des Dragons (dragoons)
17ème Régiment des Dragons
18ème Régiment des Dragons
19ème Régiment des Dragons
27ème Régiment des Dragons
CORPS ARTILLERY: (nine 12pdrs)
Note: Gudin's 3rd Division of III Corps never reached the battlefield, but part of Caffarelli's (*vice* Bisson) 1st appeared later. Also, the *1er Régiment de Dragons* was attached independently to I Corps.
Strength at Austerlitz: 6,300 men (including 2,500 cavalry) and 12 guns.

IV Corps Marshal Nicolas Jean de Dieu Soult
1ST DIVISION: General of Division Louis Vincent Le Blond de Saint-Hilaire
10ème Régiment d'Infanterie Légère
14ème Régiment d'Infanterie de Ligne
36ème Régiment d'Infanterie de Ligne
2ND DIVISION: General of Division Dominique Joseph René Vandamme
24ème Régiment d'Infanterie Légère
4ème Régiment d'Infanterie de Ligne
28ème Régiment d'Infanterie de Ligne
43ème Régiment d'Infanterie de Ligne
46ème Régiment d'Infanterie de Ligne
55ème Régiment d'Infanterie de Ligne
57ème Régiment d'Infanterie de Ligne
3RD DIVISION: General of Division Claude Juste Alexandre Legrand
26ème Régiment d'Infanterie Légère
3ème Régiment d'Infanterie de Ligne
18ème Régiment d'Infanterie de Ligne
75ème Régiment d'Infanterie de Ligne
Tirailleurs du Pô (Italian light infantry)
Tirailleurs Corses (Corsican light infantry)
LIGHT CAVALRY DIVISION: General of Brigade Pierre Margaron
8ème Régiment de Hussards (Hussars)
11ème Régiment de Chasseurs à Cheval
26ème Régiment de Chasseurs à Cheval
CORPS ARTILLERY: 35 guns (mostly 12pdrs)
Strength at Austerlitz: 23,600 men and 35 guns.

V Corps Marshal Jean Lannes
1ST DIVISION: General of Division Marie François Auguste Caffarelli
13ème Régiment d'Infanterie Légère
17ème Régiment d'Infanterie de Ligne
30ème Régiment d'Infanterie de Ligne
51ème Régiment d'Infanterie de Ligne
61ème Régiment d'Infanterie de Ligne
3RD DIVISION: General of Division Louis Gabriel Suchet
17ème Régiment d'Infanterie Légère
34ème Régiment d'Infanterie de Ligne
40ème Régiment d'Infanterie de Ligne
64ème Régiment d'Infanterie de Ligne
88ème Régiment d'Infanterie de Ligne
LIGHT CAVALRY DIVISION: General of Brigade Anne François Trelliard
9ème Régiment de Hussards
10ème Régiment de Hussards
13ème Chasseurs à Cheval
21ème Chasseurs à Cheval
CORPS ARTILLERY: 20 guns (mostly 12pdrs)
Note: Gazan's 2nd Division had been transferred to Mortier's new VIII Corps earlier in the campaign.
Strength at Austerlitz: 12,700 men and 20 guns.

Grenadier Division General of Division Nicolas Charles Oudinot
Note: this famous provisional formation was made up from élite companies of regiments still forming in France or on garrison duty as follows:
Carabinier companies (equivalent to grenadiers in light infantry formations) from:
2ème, 3ème, 15ème, 28ème and *31ème Régiments d'Infanterie Légère*
Grenadier companies from: *9ème, 13ème, 58ème* and *81ème Régiments d'Infanterie de Ligne*
Strength at Austerlitz: 5,700 men.

Cavalry Reserve Marshal Prince Joachim Murat
FIRST HEAVY CAVALRY DIVISION: General of Division Etienne Nansouty
1er Régiment de Carabiniers à Cheval (wore no armour)
2ème Régiment de Carabiniers à Cheval
2ème Régiment de Cuirassiers (wore breast- and back-plates)
3ème Régiment de Cuirassiers
9ème Régiment de Cuirassiers
12ème Régiment de Cuirassiers

SECOND HEAVY CAVALRY DIVISION: General of Division Jean d'Hautpoul
1er Régiment de Cuirassiers
5ème Régiment de Cuirassiers
10ème Régiment de Cuirassiers
11ème Régiment de Cuirassiers
SECOND DRAGOON DIVISION: General of Division Frederic Henri Walther
3ème Régiment de Dragons
6ème Régiment de Dragons
10ème Régiment de Dragons
11ème Régiment de Dragons
13ème Régiment de Dragons
22ème Régiment de Dragons
THIRD DRAGOON DIVISION: General of Division Marc Antoine Beaumont
5ème Régiment de Dragons
8ème Régiment de Dragons
12ème Régiment de Dragons
16ème Régiment de Dragons
21ème Régiment de Dragons
LIGHT CAVALRY DIVISION: General of Division François Etienne Kellermann
2ème Régiment de Hussards
4ème Régiment de Hussards
5ème Régiment de Hussards
5ème Régiment de Chasseurs à Cheval
LIGHT CAVALRY BRIGADE: General of Brigade Edouard Jean Milhaud
16ème Régiment de Chasseurs à Cheval
22ème Régiment de Chasseurs à Cheval
Attached Artillery: 36 guns in companies of *artillerie à cheval*
Note: parts of the Cavalry Reserve were detached for service with various *corps d'armée* according to requirement.
Strength at Austerlitz: 7,400 sabres and 36 guns.

The Army Trains three battalions of *train d'artillerie,* responsible for horse teams and drivers hauling the cannon and a large number of other supporting tasks.
Strength at Austerlitz: 3,000 men.

Overall Strength of La Grande Armée d'Allemagne at Austerlitz
After allowing for detachments, stragglers and sick, it is estimated that approximately 73,000 men of all arms and 139 cannon fought on 2 December 1805.

Bavarian infantry, 1806–14, by A. Hoffmann. Another new French ally was Bavaria, which also formed a division for the Reserve Corps in 1805 under General Deroy. Bavarian infantry were noted for their sky-blue uniform coats and distinctive headgear. Here a variety of types are depicted (from left to right): a first lieutenant and a grenadier; a corporal and a drummer; a fusilier, a second lieutenant and a sharp-shooter – wearing the distinctive tassel. Bavaria proved a staunch French ally until 1813. (Anne S. K. Brown Military Collection, Brown University)

There were also battalions of train troops responsible for moving up ammunition, food and other stores, as well as for supplying drivers and horse teams for the artillery. However, the French believed in keeping convoys to a minimum size and relied upon the troops being able to supplement a meagre diet by 'living off the countryside'. This is what made possible the fast, sustained marching that so mesmerized France's opponents, and which the corps system was designed to maximize by spreading the line of advance over as wide an area as was conversant with security in order to ease the load on particular roads and also broaden the area of country available for foraging.

The Imperial Guard, 7,000 strong for the campaign of Austerlitz, was the élite organization of the whole army, and comprised infantry, cavalry, artillery and services. This famous formation had evolved from the Guard of the Directory and the Consular Guard, together with General Bonaparte's mounted *Guides* of 1796. With great esteem and privileges and pay to match, service in the Guard was much sought after, and used as a reward for valorous conduct.

The men of the *Grande Armée* were in the main provided by conscription. All men between the ages of 18 and 40 were required to register; those of between 18 and 25 (later 30) were liable for call-up for unlimited service in annual classes; sometimes selection by drawing lots was resorted to, mainly after 1805. In later years conscription would be hated and feared, but in 1805 there was much enthusiasm still evident. More soldiers were provided by foreign contingents (thus in 1805 from Bavaria and Württemberg) and in later years from a wide range of European countries, mostly unwillingly.

Napoleon could never have enough officers, and from *maréchal de l'empire* (of whom there were 18 in 1805) to *sous-lieutenant*, or subaltern, there was a strict promotion system. Many officers emerged from the ranks, others were provided by *l'Ecole Spéciale Militaire de Saint-Cyr*, founded in 1802 for training infantry and cavalry, and by *l'Ecole Polytechnique* for engineers and gunners. As events in 1805 showed, the concept of *la carrière ouverte aux talents* could produce officers of the desired standard.

To control and synchronize there was *le-Grand-Quartier-Général*, or Imperial Headquarters. Napoleon devised his own staff organization. In 1805 it numbered 400 officers and 5,000 men (to include its escort). The staff comprised three main sections. First there was the *Maison*, Napoleon's personal headquarters, itself divided into several parts: the Emperor's Cabinet,

*French Hussar Officer,
c.1805. A hussar of the
Third Regiment of
Hussars, wearing the
typical cavalry shako and
fur-trimmed pelisse, or
undress jacket, which was
often worn in dashing
style slung from the left
shoulder. The sabretache,
or cavalry officer's satchel
worn on long straps from
the left of his waistbelt,
was embellished with the
regimental number and
other designations. (Anne
S. K. Brown Military
Collection, Brown
University)*

*Württemberg light
infantryman, by Ebner. In
1805 the Elector of
Württemberg was pressed
to send a contingent to
support the Grande
Armée, and in due course
a division was formed
under General Seeger
which formed part of the
Reserve Corps. Light
infantrymen, or jaegers,
often carried shorter
muskets (as shown here)
than line infantry. (Anne
S. K. Brown Military
Collection, Brown
University)*

which included the key nerve-centre, the *Bureau Topographique* (or Map Office), run by Bacler d'Albe and a dozen key advisers; the Emperor's Household (officers, aides, servants, secretaries, valets and cooks, who looked after Napoleon's well-being) run by Marshal-of-the-Palace Duroc; and his 'little headquarters' or tactical HQ, a dozen key officers under Chief-of-Staff Berthier who accompanied Napoleon at all times. The General Headquarters (also ruled by Marshal Berthier) comprised four major *bureaux* or offices, each with its own staff and special duties. Thirdly there was the Administrative Headquarters, run by Daru, often operating from well to the rear and specializing in logistics. There was also a group of other headquarters, including those of Foreign Affairs and the Imperial Guard, the Artillery and the Engineers. Miniaturized headquarters, reflecting the *GQG*, were to be found at corps and, smaller yet, at divisional levels.

The Austrian Army

The Austrian army of 1805 was in large measure the creation of 'the unfortunate General Mack', the out-generalled commander of the Emperor Francis II's army at Ulm. A Protestant – something of a rarity in itself in Catholic Austria – he had emerged

to note in 1794 by writing *Instructions for Generals*, which stressed the all-importance of the offensive in campaigning. Five years later his reputation had taken a severe dent while commanding the Army of the Two Sicilies in Naples, a force about whom their realistic Bourbon monarch had remarked (of a proposed change of uniform in the interests of engendering higher morale), 'Dress them in red, blue or green – they'll run away just the same.' Taken prisoner by the French, he had broken parole to return to Holy Russia. However, he had re-emerged from deserved obscurity in 1805 as the war clouds began to gather, and on 22 April had been appointed Chief of Staff (or Quartermaster-General, in Austrian terminology). This was a setback for the Archduke Charles, undoubtedly the ablest Habsburg commander of his generation, whose influence on the Aulic Council, or *Hofkriegsrath* (the Court War Council), an assembly of august grey-beards with supreme authority second only to that of their Emperor (a monarch with no claim whatsoever to military pretensions) over all matters pertaining to strategy. Certainly, as we have seen, Charles was awarded command of the army in north Italy – supposedly the most likely scene of decisive conflict in at least Vienna's estimation – but the impressive optimism of Mack brought him command of the Danube army with

THE ALLIED ARMY

Nominal Commanders-in-Chief: The Tsar Alexander I and the Emperor Francis II
Field Commander: General Mikhail Hilarionovich Golenischev-Kutusov
Austrian Force Commander: Lieutenant-General Prince Johann von Lichtenstein
Austrian Chief of Staff: Major-General Weyrother

The Russian Imperial Guard Grand Duke Constantine
INFANTRY OF THE GUARD:
Ismailovsky Regiment of Life Guards (two battalions)
Semenovsky Regiment of Life Guards (two battalions)
Preobrazhensky Regiment of Life Guards (two battalions)
Guard *Jaeger* Battalion (light infantry)
Guard Grenadier Regiment (three battalions)
CAVALRY OF THE GUARD:
Chevalier Guard Cuirassier Regiment (five squadrons)
The *Garde du Corps* Cuirassier Regiment (five squadrons)
Lifeguard Hussar Regiment (five squadrons)
Lifeguard Cossack Regiment (two squadrons)
Pioneers of the Guard (one company)
Strength at Austerlitz: 6,730 infantry, 3,700 horsemen, 100 Pioneers and 40 guns (mostly attached to regiments)

Advance Guard of the Tsar's Army Lieutenant-General Peter I. Bagration
INFANTRY FORMATIONS:
5th *Jaeger* Regiment (three battalions)
6th *Jaeger* Regiment (three battalions)
Arkhangelgorod Regiment (three battalions)
Old Ingermanland Infantry Regiment (three battalions)
Pskov Infantry Regiment (3 batalions)
CAVALRY FORMATIONS:
The Empress Cuirassier Regiment (five squadrons)
Tver Dragoon Regiment (five squadrons)
St Petersburg Dragoon Regiment (three squadrons)
Pavlograd Hussar Regiment (ten squadrons)
Mariupol Hussar Regiment (ten squadrons)
Kiselev Cossack Regiment (five squadrons)

Malakhov Cossack Regiment (five squadrons)
Khaznenkov Cossack Regiment (five squadrons)
Strength at Austerlitz: 9,200 infantry, 4,500 horsemen and 42 guns (mostly attached to regiments).

Advance Guard of General Frederick William Buxhöwden's Command General Kienmayer
1ST INFANTRY BRIGADE: Major-General Carneville
The Broder Infantry Regiment (one battalion)
1st Székler Infantry Regiment (two battalions)
2nd Székler Infantry Regiment (two battalions)
Pioneers (three companies)
1ST (MIXED) CAVALRY BRIGADE: Major-Generals Stutterheim and Nostitz
The O'Reilly Regiment of *Chevaulégers* (eight squadrons)
Merveldt *Uhlan* Regiment (one troop of lancers)
Schwarzenberg *Uhlan* Regiment (two troops)
Hessen-Homburg Hussar Regiment (six squadrons)
2ND CAVALRY BRIGADE: Major-General Moritz Lichtenstein
Székler Hussar Regiment (eight squadrons)
Sysoev Cossack Regiment (five squadrons)
Melentev Cossack Regiment (five squadrons)
Strength at Austerlitz: 3,440 infantry, 3,440 horsemen and 12 light guns.

First Column Lieutenant-General Dmitri Sergeivich Doctorov
1ST (MIXED) INFANTRY BRIGADE: Major-General Lewis
7th *Jaeger* Regiment (one battalion)
New Ingermanland Infantry Regiment (three battalions)
Yaroslav Infantry Regiment (two battalions)
2ND INFANTRY BRIGADE: Major-General Urusov
Vladimir Infantry Regiment (three battalions)
Bryansk Infantry Regiment (three battalions)
Vyatka Infantry Regiment (three battalions)
Moscow Infantry Regiment (three battalions)
Kiev Grenadier Regiment (three battalions)
Pioneers (one company)
ATTACHED CAVALRY:
Denisov Cossack Regiment (part: two and a half squadrons present)
Strength at Austerlitz: 13,240 infantry, 250 cavalry, 40 light and 24 heavy guns.

Second Column Lieutenant-General A. Langeron
1ST INFANTRY BRIGADE: Major-General Olsuvev
8th *Jaeger* Regiment (two battalions)
Viborg Infantry Regiment (two battalions)
Perm Infantry Regiment (three battalions)
Kursk Infantry Regiment (three battalions)
2ND INFANTRY BRIGADE: Major-General I. S. M.
Kaminsky
Ryazan Infantry Regiment (three battalions)
Fanagoria Grenadier Regiment (three battalions)
Pioneers (one company)
ATTACHED CAVALRY:
St Petersburg Dragoon Regiment (two squadrons)
Isayev Cossack Regiment (one squadron)
Strength at Austerlitz: 11,250 infantry, 300
horsemen, and 30 light guns.

Third Column Lieutenant-General I. Przbyswski
1ST (AUSTRIAN) INFANTRY LIGHT BRIGADE:
Major-General Müller
7th *Jaeger* Regiment (two battalions)
8th *Jaeger* Regiment (one battalion)
2ND (MIXED) INFANTRY BRIGADE: Major-General
Selekhov
Galicia Infantry Regiment (three battalions)
Butyrsk Infantry Regiment (three battalions
Podolia Infantry Regiment (three battalions)
Narva Infantry Regiment (three battalions)
Pioneers (one company)
Strength at Austerlitz: 7,700 infantry and 30 light
guns.

Fourth Column Lieutenant-Generals M. A.
Miloradovich and J. K. Kollowrath
ADVANCE GUARD: Lieutenant-Colonel Monakhtin
Novgorod Infantry Regiment (part: two battalions)
Apsheron Infantry Regiment (part: one battalion)
Archduke John Dragoon Regiment (two
squadrons)
1ST INFANTRY BRIGADE: Major-General
Wodniansky
Novgorod Infantry Regiment (part: one battalion)
Apsheron Infantry Regiment (part: two battalions)
Little Russia Grenadier Regiment (three battalions)
Smolensk Infantry Regiment (three battalions)
2ND (AUSTRIAN) INFANTRY BRIGADE: Major-
General Rottermund
Salzburg Infantry Regiment (six battalions)
Kaunitz Infantry Regiment (one battalion)
Auersperg Infantry Regiment (one battalion)

3RD (AUSTRIAN) INFANTRY BRIGADE: Major-
General Jurczik
Kaiser Infantry Regiment (one battalion)
Czartoryski Infantry Regiment (one battalion)
Reuss-Gratz Infantry Regiment (one battalion)
Württemberg Infantry Regiment (one battalion)
Beaulieu Infantry Regiment (one battalion)
Kerpen Infantry Regiment (one battalion)
Lindenau Infantry Regiment (one battalion)
Vienna *Jaeger* (two companies)
Pioneers (two companies)
Total present at Austerlitz: 23,900 infantry, 52 light
and 24 heavy guns.

Fifth (Cavalry) Column Lieutenant-General
Prince Johann von Lichtenstein
1ST (AUSTRIAN) CAVALRY BRIGADE: Major-
General Caramelli
Nassau Cuirassier Regiment (six squadrons)
Lothringen Cuirassier Regiment (six squadrons)
2ND (AUSTRIAN) CAVALRY BRIGADE: Major-
General Weber
Kaiser Cuirassier Regiment (eight squadrons)
3RD (MIXED) CAVALRY BRIGADE: Major-General
Gladkov
Grand Duke Constantine *Uhlan* Regiment (ten
squadrons)
Gordeev Cossack Regiment (five squadrons)
Isayev Cossack Regiment (four squadrons)
Denisov Cossack Regiment (part: two and a half
squadrons)
4TH CAVALRY BRIGADE: General-Adjutant F. P.
Uvarov
Chernigov Dragoon Regiment (five squadrons)
Kharkov Dragoon Regiment (five squadrons)
Elisabetgrad Hussar Regiment (ten squadrons)
Total present at Austerlitz: 5,375 horsemen, 24 light
pieces.

**Overall Strength of the Allied (Russo-
Austrian) Army at Austerlitz**
After allowing for detachments, stragglers and sick,
it is estimated that approximately 85,400 men of all
arms (with 278 cannon) fought on 2 December
1805.

GENERAL NOTE: except where labelled 'Austrian'
or 'mixed' above, all formations are to be taken as
'Russian'.

special and specific responsibilities for cooperation with the Russian ally.

What Mack actually found on assuming command as Chief of Staff would have daunted a more realistic general. More than a decade of unsuccessful wars stretching back to 1792 had almost bankrupted the state, and defence spending had been halved as recently as 1804 – and many of the 350,000 troops nominally on the establishment had been disbanded to save their pay. The wagon-trains and artillery teams had been broken up as a further economy.

Austrian infantry. Left to right: Drummer, German fusiliers; Officer, Hungarian grenadiers;

NCO, German grenadiers. Illustrations by Bryan Fosten.

To his credit, Mack had at once set to work to repair some of the damage. The aristocratic cavalry (possibly 58,000 strong, at least on paper) was the most satisfactory part of the army. It comprised eight regiments of partly armoured cuirassiers, six of dragoons, as many of light dragoons (or *chevaulégers*), twice that number of hussars and three of lancers. Most regiments had an establishment of eight squadrons, but these varied from 160 horsemen apiece in the 'heavies' to some 210 in the light cavalry. As the scion of a very minor Franconian family, it behoved Mack to tread warily

Austrian cavalry. Left to right: 'German' cavalry trooper in undress; Trumpeter, 5th Hussars, full dress; Wachtmeister, 4th Hussars, full dress. Illustrations by Bryan Fosten.

Austrian senior officers, by R. Ottenfeld. An Austrian general (centre) receives a report from a staff officer. In rear a 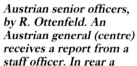 *regiment of grenadiers is drawn-up. Many Austrian field uniforms were white-grey in colour. (Author's collection)*

Austrian cavalry, after R. von Ottenfeld. An officer (foreground) and trooper (rear) of Austrian cuirassiers of the type that served under Lieutenant-General Hohenlohe's command at Austerlitz as part of *Prince Lichtenstein's Fifth Column. Three regiments of Austrian cuirassiers were present – the Nassau, Lothringen and Kaiser Regiments (20 squadrons in all). (Philip J. Haythornthwaite)*

among the holders of great titles and vast estates in the Empire who were the most influential cavalry commanders, but he did insist on a reduction of the habitual battle formation to two ranks. For the rest, he left well alone.

The Habsburg infantry he felt more confident about reforming. The 'curse of Babel' was insoluble in an army that drew its rank and file from the peasantries of a vast and multi-national empire. The basis of the infantry were the regiments (still with colonel-proprietors), the largest permanent formations that would be grouped in *ad hoc* 'columns' or brigades as need arose. Here Mack set to work with a reformer's zeal, and with the Emperor's blessing in June 1805 he imposed a standardized establishment. Each regiment was to comprise one battalion of grenadiers and four more of line infantry, each battalion to be made up of four companies. Allowing for a smaller grenadier

establishment of 600 men to the more usual 800 soldiers in a line battalion, this theoretically produced a regiment of over 3,800 officers and men. But even Mack's undeniable energy and flood of paper instructions and new regulations could not overcome three major problems. First, his new regulations were only issued in June 1805, and so war caught the Austrian army in the midst of implementing the changes: as a result some regiments had conformed, others not, and a conservative colonel was in a position virtually to ignore any changes he disapproved of amid the chaos of mobilization for war. Second, the army was equipped with a flintlock musket, or *flinte*, dating from 1754 (that of the French opponent dated from 1777 and was considerably superior).

Austrian infantry, after J. B. Seele. An officer of a German fusilier company (right) speaks to Hungarian fusiliers (left) and a Hungarian grenadier (wearing the peakless grenadier bearskin cap). The Austrian Empire always distinguished between 'German' and 'Hungarian' enlisted troops. (Philip J. Haythornthwaite)

period as skirmishers after the French pattern already described above. Indeed, it was the rigidity of Austrian tactical concepts that formed one of their greatest weaknesses. Formal linear tactics of the 18th century type enforced by a strict discipline produced what were jocularly described as 'walking muskets'. Not even officers dared break away from the dead hand of the regulations, and Mack's well-meant intended tactical reforms came far too late to redeem the situation by the later months of 1805. The Austrians continued to place their faith in platoon, company or battalion volleys, delivered by formations drawn up three or four ranks deep in their distinctive white uniforms.

The Austrian artillery was another relic of a greater past in the 1750s. Organized into four regiments of sixteen companies (or batteries) apiece, it numbered barely 11,000 men all told. Drafts from infantry regiments were continually used to make up the gun-crews. Horses to draw the cumbersome pieces (far weightier than the French guns of the Gribeauval reforms had to be pressed into service from civilian sources each time war threatened. In 1805 the complement was only at half strength. Lighter cannon were invariably attached to infantry regiments and thus strong batteries were rarely organized, although some heavier pieces were trained in the Artillery Reserve. The standard guns were 3pdr, 6pdr and 12pdr cannon and 7pdr howitzers, but in every case their calibre was less than that of the French (lighter) equivalent. As for supply, Mack was dazzled by Napoleon's reputation, and attempted to copy the French system (unsatisfactory though it often was) of 'living off the countryside'. His quartermasters drew a great sigh of relief and promptly refused to issue not only food but even remounts and uniforms in some instances. In 1792, Austrian armies had always marched with at least nine days' rations in cumbrous, slow-moving wagons. Now, in 1805, they moved even more slowly through a general shortage of horse teams but often without any rations. Even worse, their Russian allies were largely dependent on the Austrians for their supplies – even down to boots, shoes and tentage. The results can be imagined.

The Army Staff was – on paper – meticulously organized thanks to the earlier efforts of Field

And, third, Mack could in no way influence the traditional Habsburg love for changing the composition of 'columns' or 'corps' on almost a weekly basis – which meant that no general ever knew his troops. It was one thing for Napoleon to create new *corps d'armée* in mid-campaign (as we have already seen in the case of Mortier's VIII Corps in late 1805), but quite another for the Austrians to make frequent changes at lower levels (which Napoleon never did, his divisions and regiments remaining constant in organization and grouping). The end-result was a chaos that astounded even the Tsar's generals.

But not all was hopeless in the Habsburg infantry. The Croatian light infantry from the *militargrenze* or 'military frontiers' were enthusiastic and redoubtable fighters, but unfortunately they were under-trained and never employed at this

Marshal Lacy and proved unsurpassed in the production of paper and paperwork. Few armies have ever been so bedevilled with demands for so many daily returns to higher authority. As for military intelligence, its standard may be judged from the basic failure to comprehend the difference between the Russian and European calendars. But the Army Staff was efficient in providing guides, although this led to much friction with their Russian allies, who did not appreciate being told how to comport themselves on the march.

Thus, behind an ostensibly impressive military façade, all was 'mildewed' in the Austrian army. It would see better days after 1805 when the gifted Archduke Charles and his relatively competent brothers received a freer hand to redesign the army, but in 1805 there was little hope for the Habsburgs against Napoleon's magnificent and ruthless genius. And the hard lessons of the Ulm campaign were to be applied again with even greater effect on the frost-covered fields of Moravia.

Russian infantry, after L. Ebner. This shows the Russian uniform prior to the adoption of the '1805 shako', but many units were still wearing the bicorne hat at Austerlitz. The group at the left includes an officer (with cane), a fusilier and a grenadier of a Grenadier Regiment, the last two wearing their distinctive mitre-caps. (Philip J. Haythornthwaite)

The Soldiers of Holy Russia

The Russian armies shared a fair number of the problems of their Austrian allies as well as being dependent upon them for subsistence. It had been modelled in large measure on Prussian concepts by the mad Tsar Paul I (1754–1801). His successor, the young and impressionable Alexander I, as much bedazzled by Napoleon as was General Mack, had attempted a measure of liberal army reform since 1801 but had only succeeded in confusing the situation. Thus the older commanders such as Kutusov, Buxhöwden and Bennigsen distrusted the new ideas and often chose to ignore them. The modernists around the Tsar on the other hand, such as Wintzingerode and Dolgorouki, scorned the older generation of commanders and made no attempt to conceal their feelings. This disharmony was to cost the Russians dearly between 1805 and 1807.

The Tsar did not lack manpower, with some 44 million people under his despotic rule. Most Russian men – whether serf or free – were technically liable to 25 years of military service if they were selected, and in 1805 a levy of four out of every 500 liable young men had added 110,000 recruits to the army. In overall terms, there were some 300,000 regulars in the green uniform and another 200,000 recruits (half of them Cossacks, the remainder the new conscripts of 1805). Nominally the Russian land forces were divided into eighteen so-called 'divisions', each supporting six infantry regiments of three battalions apiece, 20 cavalry squadrons (ten heavy and ten light) and 82 cannon. Included in the infantry were thirteen regiments of grenadiers and twenty *jaeger* (or light infantry) formations. From recent date all regiments were supposed to have a common establishment of 2,256 men, apart from *jaeger* units, which contained only 1,385.

A cast apart were the élite formations of the Russian Imperial Guard. In the year of Austerlitz this comprised six regiments of cavalry, one battalion of *jaeger*, and three regiments of Guards, namely the Preobrazhensky (3,000 strong), the Semenovsky and the Ismailovsky (each with 2,264 men). The tallness of the selected soldiers was enhanced by their brass-fronted mitre caps, and

1, Russian infantry. Musketeer Officer, Lithuania Regiment; 2, Private, Semenovski Lifeguard; 3, Musketeer, Rostov Regiment; 4, Musketeer Sergeant, Ukraine Regiment. Illustrations by Paul Hannon.

their commanders were the cream of the officer-class in terms of ability, valour and social standing.

The average Russian soldier was noted to be tough and brave, often fatalist in outlook, but totally devoid of education, poorly-uniformed, indifferently armed and appallingly paid. On occasion, he was liable to get out of control, and at such moments he resorted to sheer barbarity. But mostly the *moujik*-soldiery were noted for great physical endurance, loyalty to their officers and above all to 'the Little Father' (the Tsar), frankness and respect for their seniors, the best of whom treated them paternally, like overgrown children.

The Russian cavalryman was generally well-mounted and quite as good as his French or Austrian counterpart, while the Cossack, armed with lance, sword and pistol, was in many ways superior to the average French hussar, man for man, when properly led. In 1803, two years before Austerlitz, the Tsar had carried through considerable changes in the mounted arm. The number of cuirassier 'heavy' regiments was reduced to six and those of 'maids-of-all-work' dragoons increased to 22. Both cuirassier and dragoon regiments shared an establishment of five two-company (troop) squadrons, making a regimental strength in the region of 1,000 horsemen apiece. Turning to consider the light cavalry, one regiment of hussars had been converted to *uhlans* (or lancers) in 1802, but this formation and seven more of hussars remained the regular light cavalry component, making eight regiments in all as before. The hussar regiment's establishment was fixed at ten squadrons, each of some 190 officers and men, making 1,900 in all per formation. Additionally there were swarms of irregular horsemen, the celebrated Cossacks – perhaps as many as 100,000 in all – raised only in time of actual hostilities, when they were recruited from the regions near the River Don (above all), but also from near the River Bug, the Urals and Siberia, not to forget the south-western Steppes and the Black Sea coast. While the line cavalry were trained to fight in two ranks against formed, mounted opponents, delivering attacks which built up from the walk to the all-out charge in much the same fashion as the French cavalry, the Russian

horsemen were practised in attacking enemy infantry in smaller detachments. As for Cossack tactics, these are possibly most accurately described as 'swarm' envelopments of enemy flanks in battle, together with 'hit and run' missions. Their greatest fame (or notoriety) was earned as looters ravaging the enemy countryside.

As for the Russian artillerymen, they too shared a fair reputation; their horse-teams were sturdy and permanent, far better organized than the Austrian, and the gunners were generally proficient. As to their equipment, the reforms of General Arakcheev (begun in 1802) had started to take effect. Many changes were modelled on those of Gribeauval in the France of the 1780s, producing lighter and more dependable guns but a wider range of types. Thus the Russians had 6 and 12pdrs in two versions, one light, the other medium, besides a range of 3, 10 and 20pdr 'unicorns' (long barrelled howitzers instantly recognizable by the tapering of the barrel's rear next to the cascabel). Artillery companies were light or heavy and generally comprised a dozen cannon. A mixed artillery regiment, of which there were eight, held some 2,000 artillerymen organized into between four and seven companies. But in 1805 they were generally outclassed by the French artillery in terms of range and employment. Like the Austrians, the Russians tended to scatter their cannon throughout the regiments, making little attempt to form massed batteries capable of concentrated fire – although Austerlitz would hold one exception to this general rule, as will be seen.

The weakest component of the Russian army – however repugnant to admirers of the gallant military families of Tolstoi's '*War and Peace*' – was its officering. Some few, such as Generals Bagration, Doctorov and Miloradovitch, were capable and well-trained men, but many more were ignorant liabilities or socialite fops. It is interesting to quote Soviet propaganda of the 1950s supposedly describing the typical British officer of NATO, which may well reflect the commonly held view of all too many of their own early 19th century Tsarist officers:

'The English [read Russian] officer is least of all an officer. He is a rich landowner, capitalist or merchant and only an officer incidentally. He

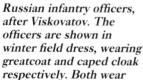

Russian infantry officers, after Viskovatov. The officers are shown in winter field dress, wearing greatcoat and caped cloak respectively. Both wear bicorne hats, which remained officer-wear long after the introduction of the shako in 1805. (Philip J. Haythornthwaite)

Russian grenadier drummer and musician, after Viskovatov. Both soldiers wear the 1805 shako, which may have been issued in time to be worn by some regiments at Austerlitz. The wings on the shoulders, the lace on the sleeves, seams and breast were indicative of musician status. The collar lace, upper shako-band and white plume-summit, together with the cane (right), are NCO distinctions of rank. (Philip J. Haythornthwaite)

knows absolutely nothing about the army and the army sees him only on parades and reviews. From the professional point of view he is the most ignorant officer in Europe. But he does not enter the army to serve, only for the uniform and the glitter – the English [read Russian] uniforms are truly magnificent, cut to fit very tight. The officer has the right to consider himself irresistible to the fair-haired, blue-eyed misses and ladies. The English [read Russian] officer is a beautiful aristocrat, extremely rich, an independent sybarite and epicure. He has a spoilt, capricious and blasé character, loves pornographic literature, suggestive pictures, recherché food, strong and strange drinks.

'His chief amusements are gambling, racing and sport. He goes to bed at dawn and gets up at midday. He is usually occupied with two mistresses simultaneously – a lady of high society and a girl drawn from the ballet or opera. His income runs into several thousands, often tens of thousands, a year, of which he keeps no account, being incapable of keeping accounts. The pay he receives from the Government hardly suffices to keep him in scent and gloves. In such conditions he considers that he has the perfect right to do anything. English [read Russian] officers, especially the young ones, do absolutely no work of any kind. They spend their nights and days in clubs of extraordinary magnificence and opulence. All consider themselves equal in a club; a colonel has no scruples about borrowing money from a subaltern. Military matters interest no one; training is always left to the N.C.O.' (From the Russian periodical *Odesskiye Novosti*, published in 1950.)

Russian cavalry. Left to right: Officer, Smolensk Dragoons, full dress; Trooper, Chevalier-Garde, full dress; NCO, Little Russia Cuirassiers, full dress. Illustrations by Bryan Fosten.

A Russian Cossack, after Horace Vernet. This picture shows the traditional image of the Cossack – the famous Russian irregular light cavalryman, many of whom came from the River Don region. There were also élite Cossack formations (e.g., the Lifeguard Cossack Regiment) attached to the Russian Imperial Guard. (Philip J. Haythornthwaite)

Officer of Russian irregular cavalry, after J. A. Atkinson, 1804. This engraving is entitled a 'Cossack' but from the head-dress is more probably a depiction of a Tartar. (Haythornthwaite)

The tactics of the Tsar's armies were also outdated. Once again Prussian concepts predominated; and although the great Suvorov had shown what could be done with a well-led army, his successors (with one or two exceptions) were not so inspired. Rigid adherence to linear tactics and rolling volleys had been challenged by Suvorov's strong predilection for the use of cold steel by the infantry, and in 1805 there was rather more latitude under Kutusov's control: and the use of columnar attacks and even the dispersed skirmishing order was permissable. The cavalry were required to fight in double ranks and were trained to select their targets with care and adapt their tactics to circumstances. Cossack units specialized in wheeling attacks plying their lances.

But the weakness of much of the higher leadership and the inadequacies of the commissariat were grave liabilities for the Russians when engaged in a large-scale campaign far from their homeland, as events in late 1805 were to demonstrate only two well. The supply services were rendered hopeless through lack of both adequate transport and ready money for local purchases. Like a swarm of locusts, a Russian army ate up all resources in its vicinity and then moved on to pastures new to repeat the process. The staff was inefficient and swamped in red tape. Such then, were the Allied armies about to confront Napoleon.

THE BATTLE OF AUSTERLITZ

Aware that Bernadotte's divisions were close by, and that Davout was fast approaching from the south by dint of herculean marching, Napoleon spent the remainder of 1 December granting interviews and inspecting formations. Though ragged and hungry, the French were spoiling for the fight. The defences of the Santon hill were almost complete. Several local peasants were brought in, and the Emperor personally conducted their interrogation, standing with his back to a fire. He wished to know in minutest detail the topography of the area on his right flank. Little by little, the picture was filled in. Reports of large-scale Allied movements southwards towards Aujest Markt convinced Napoleon that the enemy was indeed conforming with his intentions. 'Before tomorrow evening this army will be mine,' he confidently asserted. Early in the evening the arrival of Marshal Davout with his staff, riding well ahead of the hard-marching General Friant, further reassured him. During the night these troops – vital for the holding of the right flank – would arrive at Raigern Abbey behind Legrand's extended right. They would be in position by eight in the morning. Napoleon decided the time was ripe to issue his Order of the Day for the morrow.

'The positions that we occupy are formidable, and while the Russians march upon our batteries I shall attack their flanks.

'Soldiers, I shall in person direct all your battalions; I shall keep out of range if, with your accustomed bravery, you carry disorder and confusion into the ranks of the enemy; but if the victory is for a moment uncertain, you shall see your Emperor expose himself in the front rank. . . .

'Note that no man shall leave the ranks under the pretext of carrying off the wounded. Let every man be filled with the thought that it is vitally necessary to conquer these paid lackeys of England who so strongly hate our nation. . . .' Run off on the

Louis Nicolas Davout. The youngest of the eighteen Marshals of the Empire appointed in 1804, Davout (1770–1823) was one (with Massena and Suchet) of the three ablest soldiers who served Napoleon. In 1805 he commanded III Corps, won the engagement of Maria Zell in Styria on 8 November and conducted a fine forced-march from Vienna to join the right flank of the Grande Armée just before the start of the battle of Austerlitz – an important factor in securing the victory. His finest hour would come in 1806 in Prussia, when single-handed he won the battle of Auerstädt in Saxony. (Anne S. K. Brown Military Collection, Brown University)

headquarters mobile press, the Order was read to every unit almost before the ink was dry.

After a simple supper in his bivouac atop the Zurlan hill overlooking Lapanz Markt, at which the Emperor was seen at his gayest while conversation flowed around literary subjects and the lure of the Orient, participants recalled later, Napoleon took a short rest. It was a chill night. Awakened by General Savary, chief of intelligence, soon after midnight with news that an enemy force had driven the *Tirailleurs du Pô* out of Telnitz at the southern extremity of the line, Napoleon called for his horse and escort, and rode south to examine the situation, taking Soult with him. Soon convinced that the problem was local, the Emperor rode on to get a better view of the enemy campfires and in the process ran into a patrol of Cossacks, necessitating a rapid canter back over to the safe side of the Goldbach. This little excitement safely over, the Emperor decided to walk through the French encampments. As the news spread, spontaneous cheering broke out from unit after unit. *C'est l'Anniversaire! Vive l'Empereur!'* Men rushed up to behold their leader. Many twisted straw into brands and lit them at campfires to form an impromptu procession, until he was moving through a double-line of torches, surrounded by his aides who joined hands to form a ring around him as he walked slowly through the exuberant soldiers. 'Look how happy he is!' exclaimed Sergeant Coignet of the Grenadiers of the Guard. 'He looked very touched,' recorded another eyewitness, and '. . . moved his hand in a characteristic gesture as if to say "Thank you".'

Across the valley, Russian sentries called their sergeants, who took one glance at the scene before

hastening away to inform their duty officers. A hurried staff conference was convened to consider whether the commotion presaged a night attack; but little by little the commotion died away. By 2.30am all was once again quiet, and both armies returned to their fires to doze fitfully or lie apprehensively awake wondering what daylight would bring. A few over-excited picquets exchanged shots near Telnitz, where the village was soon firmly reoccupied by the *3ème* Regiment, driving off some over-bold Austrian light horse in the process; but eventually silence was restored.

As the Emperor lay back on his camp-bed to take a further rest he was heard to murmur: 'This has been the finest evening of my life.' A year to the day had elapsed since Napoleon had been crowned in Notre-Dame, to the magnificent coronation mass composed for the occasion by Lully. Before the day was out, 2 December would become famed throughout France as the anniversary of an even more imposing event than that of 1804. At four in the morning the first bugles and trumpets began to sound reveille; the dawn was come, and with it the moment for the supreme testing of *la Grande Armée* and its master.

On both sides of the Goldbach stream – the effective boundary dividing the rival armies – the formations began to take up their appointed stations amid a dense fog, which reached up the Pratzen Heights. The Allies found this a problem. By General Weyrother's complex plan, com-

The eve of Austerlitz, by Dawant. In the early hours of 2 December, Napoleon's troops put on a spontaneous torchlight procession for their commander as he visited their bivouacs, shouting: 'C'est l'Anniversaire!' Exactly a year earlier Napoleon had crowned himself Emperor in Notre Dame cathedral in Paris. A few hours ahead lay the Battle of Austerlitz. (Ben Weider Collection)

Austerlitz: Situation Evening 1 December 1805

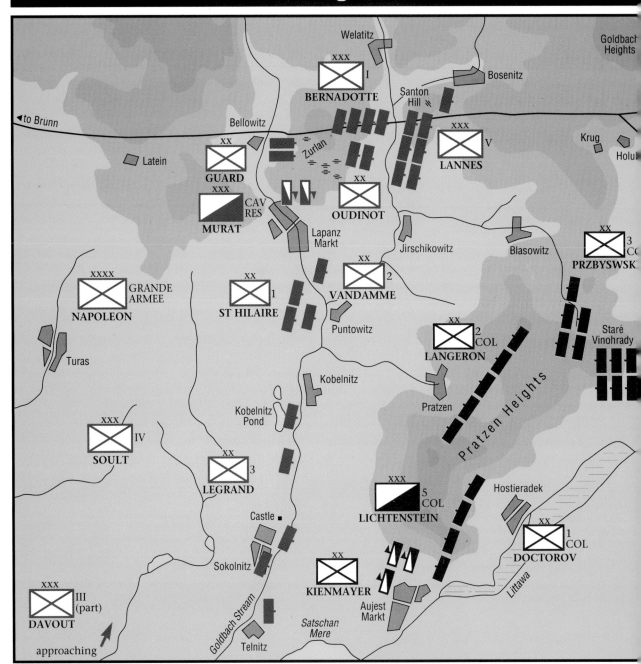

municated to the assembled staffs at Krzenowitz at 1am while Kutusov dozed, the main effort was to be made against the French right wing, to sever the road to Vienna and roll up the French northwards, while a strong secondary attack was launched up the Olmütz–Brünn highway. For the main enveloping attack, the plan called for five large bodies of troops – some 59,300 men in all – to descend into the valley under the overall command of General Buxhöwden. This force would be led by the Advance Guard under General Kienmayer, 5,100 strong. Behind him would move General Doctorov's powerful First Column (13,600), tasked with the capture of Telnitz village before swinging

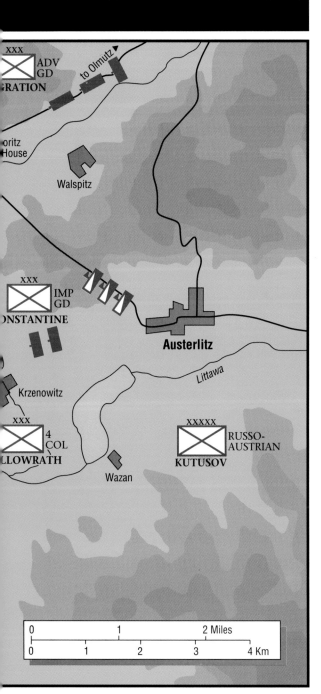

prepare for an all-out onslaught against the centre of the French line, which by this time should be bent back at right-angles holding a front running from Puntowitz to Turas. At this stage Generals Kollowrath and Langeron would debouch from the Pratzen with the Fourth Column of mixed Russian and Austrian troops (all of 23,900 men) to assault the hinge of the inverted French line at Puntowitz – the master-blow or *coup de grâce*. By this time, cavalry accompanying the Advance Guard would have swept west to cut the Brünn-Vienna high road. Meanwhile, away to the north, General Bagration was to press towards the Santon with 13,000 men, supported on his left by the Austrian Prince Lichtenstein's 4,600 cavalry linking the Allied right to the centre. In reserve would stand the Grand Duke Constantine at the head of the Guard Corps

Mounted French cuirassier. An officer of the 1st Regiment of Cuirassiers, distinguished by their tall white plumes. Note the elaborate decoration of the shabrack or saddle-cloth, a sign of commissioned rank, and the grenade symbol embroidered in the corner. Similar regiments appeared throughout Europe in imitation. Carried out by large men on heavy horses, a cuirassier charge was a daunting experience to have to face. (Anne S. K. Brown Military Collection, Brown University)

north to join General Langeron's Second Column (11,700), which would have descended from the Pratzen further north to seize Sokolnitz village, aided on his right flank by General Przbyswski's Third Column (10,000 men). At this juncture the three columns were to storm across the Goldbach and re-unite north of the lake near Kobelnitz and

Bavarian light cavalryman, 1805. Light cavalry were trained to use their carbines while mounted. Note the ramrod with attached cord designed to prevent the latter being dropped in the heat of action. (Anne S. K. Brown Military Collection, Brown University).

French heavy cavalryman. The typical French heavy cavalryman in 1805 was the cuirassier. Wearing a metal helmet embellished with horsehair plume, a breast-plate and back-plate, and armed (in the case of other ranks) with a carbine or short-barrelled cavalry musket, cuirassiers formed a major part of Murat's Cavalry Reserve. (Anne S. K. Brown Military Collection, Brown University)

(8,500 élite horse and foot) near the village of Krzenowitz. Langeron's objections that this plan would practically denude the centre on the Pratzen of troops was dismissed. Napoleon, after all, was already more than half beaten – otherwise he would surely never have abandoned the Pratzen?

In themselves these moves were complex enough, but the mist caused grave problems in the forming-up of the massive outflanking column, several parts of which unwittingly crossed each other's lines of march – and some time was taken up sorting out the confused formations. Napoleon had been roused in the early hours to receive a second report from General Savary, his chief of intelligence, who confirmed that the Allies were indeed in great strength in the vicinity of Aujest Markt and Hostieradek at the south of their line. A rapid consultation with a summoned Marshal Soult led to the dictation of few minor adjustments to the French dispositions – in particular a slight shift to the north of the start-line for the intended attack against Pratzen in order to make the most of the enemy's anticipated weakness in the centre, and the adding of 4,000 more men to strengthen Legrand's southern flank (two line regiments: the *18ème* and *75ème*; the *26ème Légère* and the *Tirailleurs du Pô* and *Corses* (light troops from North Italy and Corsica respectively) pending the arrival of Friant – and Napoleon returned to his slumbers.

His main orders had been issued the previous evening before supper but at about 5am Marshals Berthier, Soult, Lannes, Davout, Bernadotte and Prince Murat presented themselves before the Emperor's straw-floored tent to receive last-minute instructions and confirmation of his plans. Some 65,000 troops were to mass behind the Santon and in the area formed by the confluence of the Goldbach and the Bosenitz streams. Legrand (reinforced to some 12,000 men as already arranged) was to hold the right, together with Davout's 6,600 men – Friant's Division and the III Corps cavalry under Bourcier and 12 guns (three of them with the dragoon division) – whose arrival would bring the total French presence on the battlefield to 73,400 (far better odds with which to confront the Allies' 85,400 men than had existed 48 hours earlier). Friant's role was seen at this stage to be to move as far north as Turas if need arose; but in fact his men of III Corps would fight on the Goldbach sector. Lannes was to hold the Santon and its environs come what might with the 12,700 men and 20 guns of V Corps, with Murat's 5,600-strong Cavalry Reserve to guard his right flank. Bernadotte's I Corps (13,000 men and 24 guns) was to move from its concealment behind the Santon and form up between the villages of Jirschikowitz and Puntowitz, ready to attack Bläsowitz. Meanwhile Soult's remaining two divisions – those of Vandamme and Saint-Hilaire (some 16,000 men and 16 guns between them) – were to form up, concealed by the mist, on the eastern bank of the Goldbach by 7.30am ready to assault the Pratzen Heights from Puntowitz and occupy the enemy centre once the Emperor gave the signal. The Imperial Guard (5,500 men and 24 cannon) and Oudinot's grenadiers (5,700 veteran troops) were to form the army reserve. A semaphore station was being established near the Emperor's initial battle headquarters atop the Zurlan Height, with relay stations ready to pass messages by flag-signals once the coming of full daylight and the thinning of the mist allowed.

One unexpected and potentially explosive crisis was only narrowly defused. Jean Lannes arrived from the Santon shortly after Nicolas Soult. The two men had rowed with one another on 28 November, and the fiery Lannes had sent a second

The Battle of Austerlitz: Napoleon and his Staff before the battle. A near-contemporary representation; the surrounding setting of the picture is typically *'Imperial' in style, incorporating classically inspired trophies of arms. (Anne S. K. Brown Military Collection, Brown University)*

to challenge his colleague to a duel. Now the two men met for the first time since this message had been delivered. 'I thought you were a swordsman!' snarled Lannes, 'I have been waiting for you.' The officers of the staff froze in consternation. 'We have more important things to occupy our attention just now,' replied Soult loftily. Lannes shrugged his shoulders and muttered a few obscenities – but, as the eye-witness who recorded this incident, Thiébault, noted, the Marshals drew apart and the crisis was past.

A few crisp sentences from Napoleon, a few final details checked with Berthier on the map, a synchronization of time-pieces, and the meeting was over. All now being made clear, the Marshals

Austerlitz: Plans of the Opposing Armies

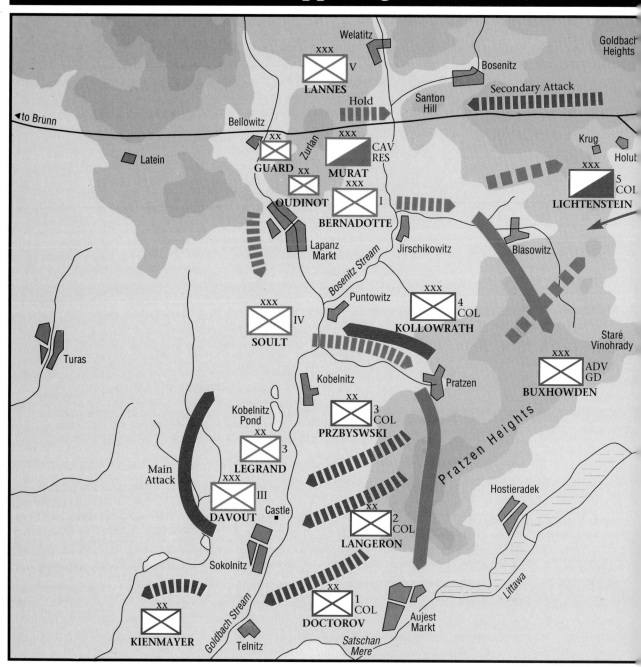

rode off to take up their respective battle stations, only Berthier and Soult remaining by the Emperor's side, a group of aides-de-camp and orderly officers forming a respectful group some yards behind. The valet Constant tried to persuade his master to take a little more breakfast, but was waved aside. The air was keen, the ground whitened over with a heavy frost. Men stood tensely to arms; horses snorted and pawed the ground; the gunners twirled their linstocks to keep them alight; *matrosses* stacked up reserves of ammunition. Tension mounted palpably.

Over the valley the mist-bound Austrians and Russians cursed and stumbled, bumping into one

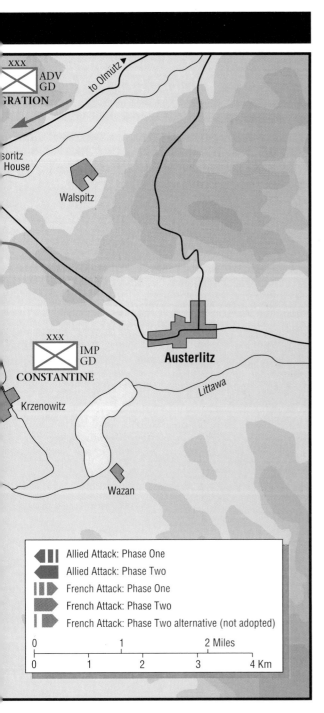

Allied Attack: Phase One
Allied Attack: Phase Two
French Attack: Phase One
French Attack: Phase Two
French Attack: Phase Two alternative (not adopted)

0   1   2 Miles
0   1   2   3   4 Km

'Mikhail Hilarionovich!' the Tsar exclaimed testily to the venerable bare-headed warrior standing at the head of his horse, 'Why haven't you begun your advance?' – a reference to the serried ranks of Generals Miloradovich's and Kollowrath's Fourth Column, who could be discerned through the mist at the halt awaiting word that the troop congestion ahead of them had been cleared. 'Your Highness,' replied Kutusov, 'I am waiting for all the columns of the army to get into position.' The Tsar was not impressed. 'But we are not on the Empress's Meadows [a parade ground near St Petersburg], where we do not begin a parade until all the regiments are formed up!' 'Your Highness,' retorted the old man, 'If I have not begun it is because we are *not* on parade, and *not* on the Empress's Meadow. However, if such be Your Highness's order. . . .' A nod sent an aide riding over to the nearby column. The imperial aides shrugged their shoulders and exchanged wondering glances at this – to them – further display of the *generalissimo*'s undue pessimism.

Buxhöwden's Onslaught

By 6am many of the Allied troops were in motion. It is true that on the right Bagration's wing remained immobile, but on the left columns of infantry, cavalry and guns were wheeling into position amid the dank, freezing fog, which delayed the coming of dawn by reinforcing the lingering shades of night. Austrian staff guides bustled to and fro as officers heaved themselves into the saddle and their men knocked out their pipes and slung their knapsacks into the regimental wagons.

At the head, Kienmayer's Advance Guard – headed by a band – left Aujest Markt and, just as the first dim light of day appeared, reached the outskirts of Telnitz village. A sharp firing broke out as the French garrison – the *Légion Corse* (familiarly known as 'the Emperor's cousins' and the *3ème Ligne* (both part of Legrand's Division of IV Corps) – aimed at the masses looming through the gloom. Well-positioned among the vineyards and houses, the French got in several telling volleys as General Stutterheim launched five battalions of Austrians – all eager to show their Russian allies what Francis II's army could achieve – in a direct attack. It failed.

another as they descended towards their designated objectives. Near the peak of Staré Vinohrady, a fur-wrapped Tsar and the Austrian Emperor, having partaken of breakfast, consulted with a reticent Kutusov, whose anxieties had evidently not been allayed by several hours' sleep. Another display of temperament ensued.

For the space of an hour the fighting around Telnitz escalated, until the French commander, discerning the approaching head of Doctorov's First Column appearing in the growing light to the north of Kienmayer's men, decided the time had come to execute his explicit orders and withdraw his massively-outnumbered 1,500 men towards Telnitz pond. Immediately 14 squadrons of Austrian cavalry bypassed the village and splashed their way to the west bank of the Goldbach. They found themselves engaged by the light horsemen of General Margaron, who in their turn gave ground upon receipt of the order, falling back northwards.

Meanwhile, Friant's Division of III Corps – which had left Gross Raigern and its abbey an hour before, much refreshed after their titanic march from Vienna by a few hours' sleep – was still on its way to support Legrand. With no idea of this coming complication, Doctorov sent back a message to General Kutusov that he had the local situation well under control and that the French were everywhere giving ground. Any minute the Russians would have found Napoleon's open flank – in other words Weyrother's plan of attack was well on the way to achieving success. But instead of pressing on, Doctorov halted his men to await the arrival of Langeron's Second Column, which for some reason appeared to be late.

The cause of this delay was a chaotic traffic jam that had developed some time before on the Pratzen. Langeron's formations had begun to move south-westwards at the appointed time when they were abruptly halted in some confusion as a mass of cavalry unceremoniously pushed their way past the head of the Second Column, moving from left to right. This major movement had been ordered by the Allied General Staff when the growing light revealed that Lichtenstein's cavalry – which were required to guard the centre – had made camp the previous evening in the wrong location. Urgent orders were immediately sent requiring Lichtenstein to transfer his horsemen to the eastern side of the Pratzen Heights without delay. The long column of trotting squadrons demanded the right of way, and it was almost an hour later before the horsemen were clear of their compatriots. Meanwhile two-thirds of Buxhöwden's vast enveloping wheel had ground to a complete halt as

Przbyswski's Third and then Kollowrath's and Langeron's Fourth Column ran into the rear of the column next ahead. For a time the confusion was indescribable. The result was the loss of a valuable hour, and it was only well after 7am that Langeron's command began to come up on the halted Doctorov's right between Telnitz and Sokolnitz.

This delay permitted Friant's men to link up with the Corsican Legion and the *3ème Ligne* behind Telnitz. Friant in person immediately launched Heudelet's Brigade in a counter-attack with the bayonet through the fog, and very soon the dumbfounded Austrians found themselves tumbled out of the village in short order and abandoning the bank of the Goldbach Stream. But the mists claimed a penalty against the French as well. As the *26ème Légère* marched south to sustain the *3ème Ligne*, it mistook the *108ème* (forming part

M. Kienmayer. Lieutenant-General Kienmayer commanded the advance guard of Doctorov's first column at Austerlitz. He was also the Austrian Chief of Staff and as such had been largely responsible for drawing up the Allied plan of battle, taking the leading role at the briefing of Austrian and Russian generals late on 1 December. (Anne S. K. Brown Military Collection, Brown University)

of Heudelet's 1st Brigade) for the enemy and opened fire. The commander of the 108ème *Ligne*, fearing himself outflanked, halted his men to return the compliment, then decided to abandon the village of Telnitz. This village was in the process of being attacked by no less than 29 Austrian and Russian units. Langeron had at last arrived on Doctorov's right and was advancing with a dozen battalions upon its target – Sokolnitz. This village also passed into Allied hands. Soon after, Przbyswski's Third Column made an appearance still further north, and began to attack Sokolnitz Castle and its walled pheasantry beyond the village of that name. Once again it seemed – however late – that Weyrother's plan was being achieved. News of

these developments reached Napoleon's signal station atop the mist-free Zurlan above Lapanz Markt – but he was unperturbed. 'Space I may recover, time never', was one of his most important maxims, and the Austrian offensive was obligingly running late.

Deluded into thinking that all was going well, the Allies began to cross to the left bank of the Goldbach. There they suddenly found themselves attacked by General Bourcier's six regiments of dragoons, closely followed by Davout in person at the head of Heudelet's infantry, who fought their way back into Telnitz and sent Doctorov's men reeling back in disorder. Without losing an instant, Friant placed himself at the head of Lochet's Brigade and, swinging his line northwards, led the *4ème* and *3ème Ligne* in a telling attack on Langeron's flank and rear, regaining possession of

Dmitri Sergeivich Doctorov. Lieutenant-General Doctorov commanded a strong Russian column of 13,650 men forming the first column of Buxhöwden's vast left wing of the Allied army, which was sent to envelop the French right flank. Bitter fighting against Legrand and later Friant failed to gain the

Goldbach valley despite the capture of Telnitz village, and it was Doctorov's command that took particularly heavy casualties around and upon the frozen meres at the close of the battle on 2 December. (Anne S. K. Brown Military Collection, Brown University)

Claude Juste Alexander Legrand. The third of Soult's divisional commanders, Legrand (1762–1815) was entrusted with the French right wing at Austerlitz, having the vital task of attracting the attentions of the vastly

stronger Allied left wing – in fact their major attack. This pinning role he carried out to perfection, aided by Friant's division of III Corps. (Anne S. K. Brown Military Collection, Brown University)

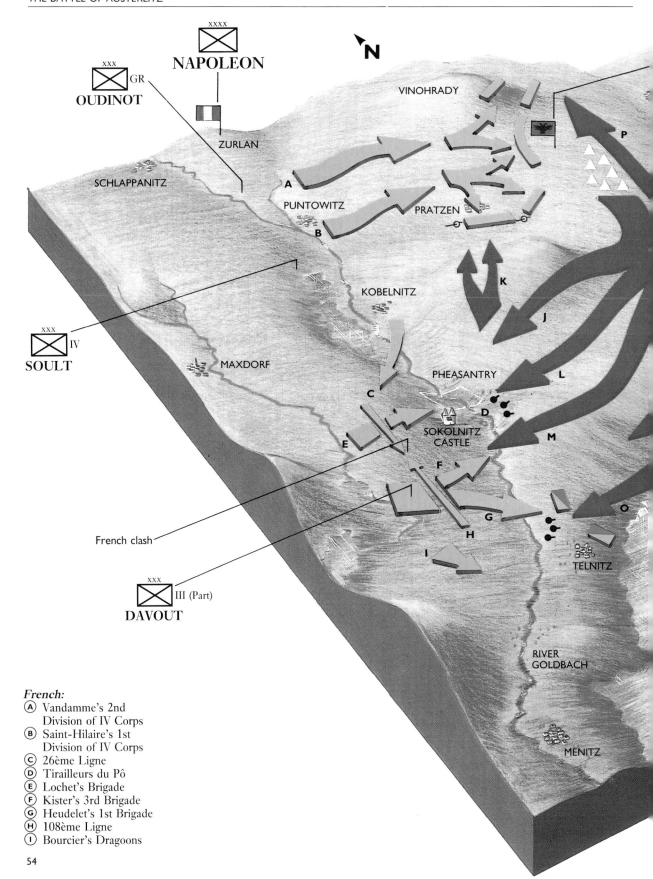

N

XXXX
NAPOLEON

XXX
OUDINOT GR

ZURLAN

VINOHRADY

SCHLAPPANITZ

A

PUNTOWITZ

B

PRATZEN

P

XXX
SOULT IV

MAXDORF

KOBELNITZ

K

J

L

PHEASANTRY

C

D

M

E

SOKOLNITZ CASTLE

F

French clash

G

H

O

I

TELNITZ

XXX
DAVOUT III (Part)

RIVER GOLDBACH

MENITZ

French:
Ⓐ Vandamme's 2nd
  Division of IV Corps
Ⓑ Saint-Hilaire's 1st
  Division of IV Corps
Ⓒ 26ème Ligne
Ⓓ Tirailleurs du Pô
Ⓔ Lochet's Brigade
Ⓕ Kister's 3rd Brigade
Ⓖ Heudelet's 1st Brigade
Ⓗ 108ème Ligne
Ⓘ Bourcier's Dragoons

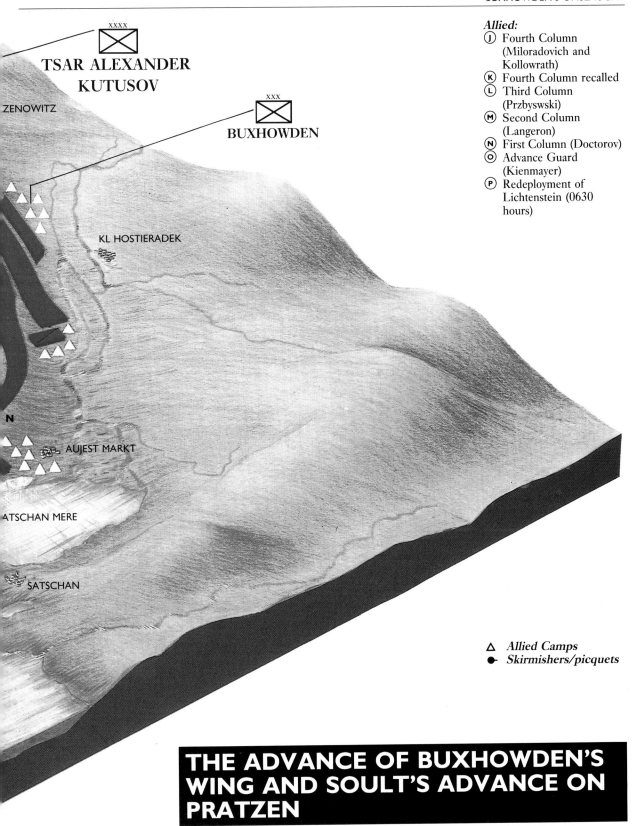

TSAR ALEXANDER
KUTUSOV

ZENOWITZ

BUXHOWDEN

KL HOSTIERADEK

N

AUJEST MARKT

ATSCHAN MERE

SATSCHAN

Allied:
- (J) Fourth Column (Miloradovich and Kollowrath)
- (K) Fourth Column recalled
- (L) Third Column (Przbyswski)
- (M) Second Column (Langeron)
- (N) First Column (Doctorov)
- (O) Advance Guard (Kienmayer)
- (P) Redeployment of Lichtenstein (0630 hours)

△ *Allied Camps*
● *Skirmishers/picquets*

THE ADVANCE OF BUXHOWDEN'S WING AND SOULT'S ADVANCE ON PRATZEN

0700 to 0900 hours

55

Louis Friant. Commander of Davout's leading division at Austerlitz, Friant (1758–1829) was the son of a wax-polisher. He became a Royal guardsman and during the Revolutionary Wars earned rapid promotion. He first served under Napoleon in 1797 and then accompanied him to Egypt. Promoted general of division in 1800 while still in the Orient, he became one of Davout's most reliable commanders. (Anne S. K. Brown Military Collection, Brown University)

the 6,000 infantry of the hard-fighting Friant) had checked, regained ground from and then defeated no less than 50,000 Allies who a short while before had been trumpetting victory. Thus, at 10am both Telnitz and Sokolnitz and the line of the Goldbach were restored to French hands. The great Allied envelopment had failed: the initiative was firmly back in French hands. As early as 1796 the then General Bonaparte had taught of the importance of a 'carefully devised defensive giving way to an all-out attack' when the moment was ripe. The defensive phase on his right flank had clearly been brilliantly achieved: it was now time to launch the counter-stroke.

The Pratzen Stormed

Napoleon had kept Marshal Soult at his side all this while, and 'the foremost manoeuvrer in Europe' found the inaction of the main part of his *corps d'armée* hard to take. Both Vandamme's and Saint-Hilaire's divisions were still concealed in the lingering thick mist in the Goldbach valley between Puntowitz and Jirschikowitz villages, and there was no sign that the foe even guessed at their presence there. The top of the Pratzen was now in sight from the Zurlan, and the Emperor's spyglass clearly revealed a torrent of the enemy moving south and downwards – perhaps already as many as 40,000, with more beginning to follow. As Napoleon intended, the Allies were obligingly emptying their centre of troops in order to execute their gigantic wheel against the French right.

At length, Napoleon turned to Soult. It was now 8.45am. 'How long will it take you to move your divisions to the top of the Pratzen Heights?' he enquired. 'Less than 20 minutes, Sire; for my troops are hidden at the foot of the valley, concealed by fog and campfire smoke.' 'In that case we will wait another quarter of an hour.' Napoleon's mind was working like a computer, calculating distances and times, odds for and against alternative courses of action, and yet leaving space for the element of 'luck'. Timing is everything in war. The Allies must be given exactly the right amount of time to clear the centre before Soult struck. As Napoleon knew, 'there is one drop of water that causes the full bucket to overflow'.

the village of Sokolnitz and flinging the enemy back to the east of the Goldbach. Leaving the *48ème* to hold Sokolnitz, the energetic Friant rode to the head of Kister's 3rd Brigade – the last uncommitted part of his division – and flung it against Przbyswski's column. Once again, and for the third time, success blessed Friant's arms and determination, and the Russians reeled back. An aide arrived with news that the *48ème* was under heavy renewed attack by Langeron. Friant immediately rode south, caught the enemy in flank yet again, and rescued his outnumbered regiment.

This period of fighting had demonstrated the fighting power of *la Grande Armée*. Just 10,300 French troops (Bourcier's 2,800 dragoons, the 1,500 men of the *3ème* of Legrand's Division and

Dominique Joseph René Vandamme. One of the toughest of Napoleon's generals, Vandamme (1770–1830) commanded another of Soult's IV Corps divisions at Austerlitz, sharing in the capture of the Pratzen Heights with Saint-Hilaire. Blunt and outspoken, he was feared by friend and foe alike, and had a predictably stormy career. His loyalty to Napoleon, however, was never questioned. (Anne S. K. Brown Military Collection, Brown University)

Nicolas Jean de Dieu Soult. The commander of IV Corps of the Grande Armée, Soult (1769–1851) was an ambitious and gifted soldier who had emerged from service in the French armies of the Rhine and of Switzerland to be created a marshal on 18 May 1804. His vital role on 2 December 1805 – especially the storming of the Pratzen Heights – caused him later to hope to be named Duke of Austerlitz; but this was a title Napoleon was prepared to award to nobody, so important did he regard this famous engagement. 'The foremost manoeuvrer in Europe', as the Emperor dubbed him, had to be content with the dukedom of Dalmatia, awarded in 1808. (Anne S. K. Brown Military Collection, Brown University)

The fifteen minutes slowly slipped away. There was the sound of heavy fighting now to the north as well as the south, for Bagration was at last engaged against Lannes along the line of the highway linking Olmütz to Brünn. The greater din, however, came from the south, where Buxhöwden was again pressing home his massive if badly delayed attack. Telnitz, as we have seen, was changing hands regularly. Heavy fighting was now taking place around Sokolnitz, its castle and pheasantry and, as Przbyswski's Third Column joined the fray in strength, towards Kobelnitz as well. But Legrand was fighting back with skill. The 26ème Légère was sent in the nick of time from Kobelnitz to reinforce the survivors of the Tirailleurs du Pô south of the enclosed park just as they were attacked by Langeron's leading brigade. The defenders of Sokolnitz rose to 1,800 men. As Przbyswski approached Kobelnitz, the Russian commander detached part of his 7th Jaeger to guard his open flank. This force found itself abruptly attacked by Levasseur's brigade of Legrand's 3rd Division issuing out of Kobelnitz – and found itself bundled back unceremoniously to the wall of the pheasantry opposite Sokolnitz Castle. Clearly, the Allies were not going to make any easier a crossing on this more northerly sector of the Goldbach than they had near hard-contended Telnitz.

The hour of nine struck from a church-tower. The time had come. Napoleon looked at Soult.

'One sharp blow and the war's over,' the Emperor said. 'I have no need to tell you what has to be done except to enjoin you to comport yourself as you always have.' But Soult had already left for the foot of the valley. So Napoleon turned to his staff officers. 'The enemy is more numerous than ourselves,' he stated, pointing with his telescope to the south. 'They expect to attack me and vanquish me. No – it's more – not only to beat us; they desire to cut us off from Vienna and round up the French army! They think I'm a novice! Well, they'll come to regret it.' At that instant the blood-red orb of the winter sun emerged as its heat dissipated the mists, and a moment later sunbeams illuminated the plain and heights. Ever thereafter men would speak of 'the sun of Austerlitz'. 'Come on!' demanded the Emperor, 'let us put an end to this campaign with a crash of thunder that will stun the enemy!' He shut his glass with a snap.

Down in the valley, drums were beating the well-known *pas de charge*, and as the spectators on the Zurlan peered down through their spyglasses they could see the glint of sunlight on a myriad bayonets as the two reserve divisions of IV Corps began to emerge from what was left of the mist, casting it aside like a dog shaking itself free from water. It was a dramatic moment as the two dense series of columns began to mount the gentle westward slopes of the Pratzen, Vandamme on the left, Saint-Hilaire on the right, without firing a shot.

Above the hamlet of Krzenowitz stood Kutusov and his headquarters staff. The latest news from the south appeared reasonably satisfactory: the French had been driven out of both Telnitz and now Sokolnitz, and yet Langeron's Second Column had mostly still to enter the fray. Reports from the north indicated a stalemate – but no matter; that was only a holding action for the Allies. But the general was still ruminating about the Tsar's brusque words as he watched Miloradovitch and Kollowrath moving south in their turn. He turned to observe the French on the hill over the valley, two kilometres away. Suddenly a staff officer let out a shout. 'My God! Look there! There, just below us – those are Frenchmen!' Kutusov started up in alarm: the enemy was only a few hundred yards away – close enough for their military bands

to be clearly heard in the still cold if now sunny and clear morning air: the strains of '*On va leur percer le flanc . . .*' were clearly distinguishable.

Kutusov knew what had to be done; the centre must immediately be reoccupied – but could it be done in time? Messengers took off new orders at a full gallop, recalling Kollowrath's Austrians and Miloradovitch's 25 Russian battalions who were descending the slope to the left towards Sokolnitz. They were to return immediately and to deploy in front of Pratzen village, facing towards Puntowitz. Then, if Prince Lichtenstein could bring up his cavalry in strength from the north. . . . But no: the Prince's newly arrived aide-de-camp made it clear that no more than four Russian mounted regiments could possibly be spared.

The Tsar had been an aghast spectator of this flurry of staff activity around him. Prince Adam Czartoryski ventured the opinion that the great Allied plan was clearly compromised beyond repair. But the cocksure Dolgorouki at once reassured his master. 'Within an hour they will all be in flight. At this very moment Doctorov and Langeron are in a position to turn their flank.' But that was not to be.

As perspiring Russian battalions doubled up-hill to protect Pratzen, they found themselves forestalled by Saint-Hilaire's division. Without deigning to respond to the uneven rattle of musketry and crash of cannon ahead of them, the French came on with the bayonet, stormed straight through the defenceless village of Pratzen without halting one moment, and attacked the Russian cannon beyond. Miloradovitch's men found themselves brushed aside. General Morand, at the head of the *10éme Léger* began to deploy into line on the plateau. General Thiébault, leading up the *14ème* and *36ème Régiments de Ligne*, suddenly found musketballs whistling into his ranks from the rear, where two Russian battalions revealed their presence in a ravine. It was the work of a moment to about-turn his men and charge these adversaries. Both Russian battalions flung down their arms in surrender. Leaving a sufficient escort, Thiébault resumed his advance eastwards in support of General Morand. Meanwhile the brigade of General Varre, part of Vandamme's 2nd Division of IV Corps, was passing to the east of Pratzen and itself making contact with the enemy, while other parts of the Division marched towards the height of Staré Vinohrady, the northern edge of the Pratzen – driving before them five Russian battalions.

From the rear, Marshal Soult adjusted his men's lines of attack. Thiébault on Saint-Hilaire's right flank, was ordered to deploy his accompanying battery of twelve guns, load with murderous canister, and sweep the Austrian ranks ahead of him. Seconds later, and the enemy were running towards the rear of the plateau. Seizing his opportunity, Vandamme marched forward in line; paused to pour several volleys into the Russian units facing him; then swept forward in a bayonet charge. The Russians did not wait to receive it, but turned and fled in their turn, disordering a second

line of Allied units who soon also ran with them, abandoning their artillery. Vandamme thereupon detached General Schiner with the *24ème Légère* to storm the Staré Vinohrady feature. In a trice another Russian battery was in French hands.

It was now 11 o'clock. Soult was master of the Pratzen Heights, placed in the precise centre of the Allied position. But would IV Corps be able to hold these gains? Kutusov was far from beaten yet – and was still of the opinion that Buxhöwden could succeed in his mission if enough time were won for him to do so. So the General busied himself reorganizing Kollowrath's and Miloradovitch's men, adding to them General Kaminski's brigade of Langeron's column, returned from Sokolnitz on its commander's own initiative once he had realized what was transpiring to the rear and centre. Moreover, the Allies still had one trump card to play: Archduke Constantine's Russian Imperial Guard, both horse and foot. Would Soult's tired but jubilant troops be able to hold on to their gains until reinforcements could arrive? Only time would tell.

The Northern Flank: Lannes against Bagration

We must turn aside from the dramatic events on the Pratzen Heights, with still more impending, to describe the battle along the axis of the Olmütz to Brünn high road, with the key Santon feature to its north. This area was the scene of the secondary major engagement.

Shortly after Marshal Lannes returned from the early-morning consultation with the Emperor, his outposts and cavalry patrols reported considerable enemy activity up the highway. By this time – shortly before 7am – the French left wing was drawn up in the formation ordered by its corps commander, with both Murat's Reserve Cavalry and Bernadotte's I Corps within supporting distance. Some of General Trelliard's corps light cavalry were about half a mile in front of the main position, acting as vedettes. Behind them were drawn up, in double-line divisional formation, the greater parts of Suchet's and Caffarelli's divisions, north and south of the main road respectively, looking east, the highway forming the divisional

Louis Vincent Saint-Hilaire. Saint-Hilaire (1766–1809) commanded one of the divisions in Soult's Corps at Austerlitz and at its head shared in the capture of the Pratzen Heights in the centre of the Allied position – the first great climax of the battle. He was wounded in the process, but recovered. More battle successes lay ahead of him until he was mortally wounded at Aspern-Essling in 1809. (Anne S. K. Brown Military Collection, Brown University)

Jean Lannes. Marshal Lannes (1769–1809) was one of Napoleon's few genuine friends and confidants, earning this special status at Arcola in 1796 where he saved the future Emperor's life. In 1805 he was given command of V Corps and at Austerlitz was entrusted with the holding of the Santon feature on the left flank of the Grande Armée. In this role he absorbed the full attention of Prince Bagration's wing of the Allied army throughout the battle. Many more distinctions lay ahead of him, but in 1809 he would be mortally wounded at the battle of Aspern-Essling and die nine days later, the first of Napoleon's Marshals to die of wounds received in action – to the Emperor's intense grief. A blunt fighting soldier with few courtly attributes, Napoleon counted him among his best battlefield commanders. (Anne S. K. Brown Military Collection, Brown University)

Marie François Auguste Caffarelli du Falga. The son of a famous engineer general (who died of wounds received at the siege of Acre in 1799), Caffarelli the Younger (1766–1849) held a divisional command in Lannes' V Corps at Austerlitz. Together with Suchet, he absorbed the attentions of the Allied right wing, ensuring the safety of the crucial Santon Hill. (Anne S. K. Brown Military Collection, Brown University)

boundary between them. On the left of Suchet guarding the open flank was the remainder of Trelliard's Light Cavalry Division, strengthened by Milhaud's Light Cavalry Brigade on detached duty from the Cavalry Reserve. Behind this cavalry the village of Bosenwitz was garrisoned by part of the *17ème Légère* (one of Suchet's formations), with the rest of that regiment garrisoning the extemporized

defences on the nearby Santon hill under General Claparède – the key pivot for the entire French left wing.

Drawn up in imposing array behind the troops so far described were the massed squadrons of Murat's Cavalry Reserve. Slotted between Suchet's second line (the *88ème* and *64ème Ligne*) and the Santon feature stood General d'Hautpoul's division of cuirassiers. South of the high road were light cavalry under General Kellermann (son of the old Marshal, the 'Victor of Valmy'), Nansouty's 'heavies' – the Carabineers and more cuirassiers, with, in reserve, General Walther's 2nd Dragoon Division. Half a mile to the south the serried ranks of Marshal Bernadotte's I Corps were discernible

Prince Joachim Murat, after Gérard. Murat (1767–1815) was the Emperor's brother-in-law (having married Caroline Bonaparte in January 1800), a Prince of the Blood and Grand Admiral of France (since February 1805). He was also the epitome of the dashing, beau sabreur *cavalry leader, whose valour on the battlefield was already legendary. He would later become King of Naples. Unfortunately his political acumen did not match his martial valour, and he would die before a firing-squad. (Philip J. Haythornthwaite)*

Peter Bagration. Of Georgian origin, Prince Bagration (1765–1812) served in the Russian army from 1782. His patron was the great Marshal Suvorov, under whom he campaigned in Switzerland and Italy in 1799. In late 1805 he was given command of the Allied right wing but was defeated, and ultimately forced to retreat, by Lannes and Murat. (Author's collection)

on the lower slopes of the Zurlan hill west of the Bosenitz stream (a tributary of the Goldbach) and behind the village of Jirschikowitz. Now that the mist had cleared away, all these dispositions were well placed to be observed from Napoleon's command post, close to which stood the formations of the Imperial Guard.

General Bagration's formations were drawn up between the hamlet of Kowalowitz and the fork where the Olmütz high road and the road to Austerlitz met near Pozorice post-house. The extreme right was entrusted to the 5th *Jaeger*. Next to the south came two lines of mounted units, light cavalry at the front (the Pavlograd and Maruipol

Hussars) with the St Petersburg, Empress's and Tver Dragoons in the second line. Close to the left of these horsemen were the Pskov and Arkhangelgorod infantry regiments, with the Old Ingermanland Regiment on its own just to the south of the high road. To the fore, loosely-organized regiments of Cossacks wheeled and darted, while on the extreme left of Bagration's so-called 'Advance Guard' (in fact the entire Allied right wing) the hamlets of Krug and Holubitz were soon garrisoned by the 6th *Jaeger* and more Cossacks. Away to the left rear were massed the squadrons of Prince Lichtenstein (once they had completed repositioning themselves as already described above), and still further to the south and out of sight to most of the Allied right wing stood the ranks of

AUSTERLITZ: OVERALL PANORAMA FROM FRENCH LEFT WING

Looking south-east and showing the main features of the battle in the north

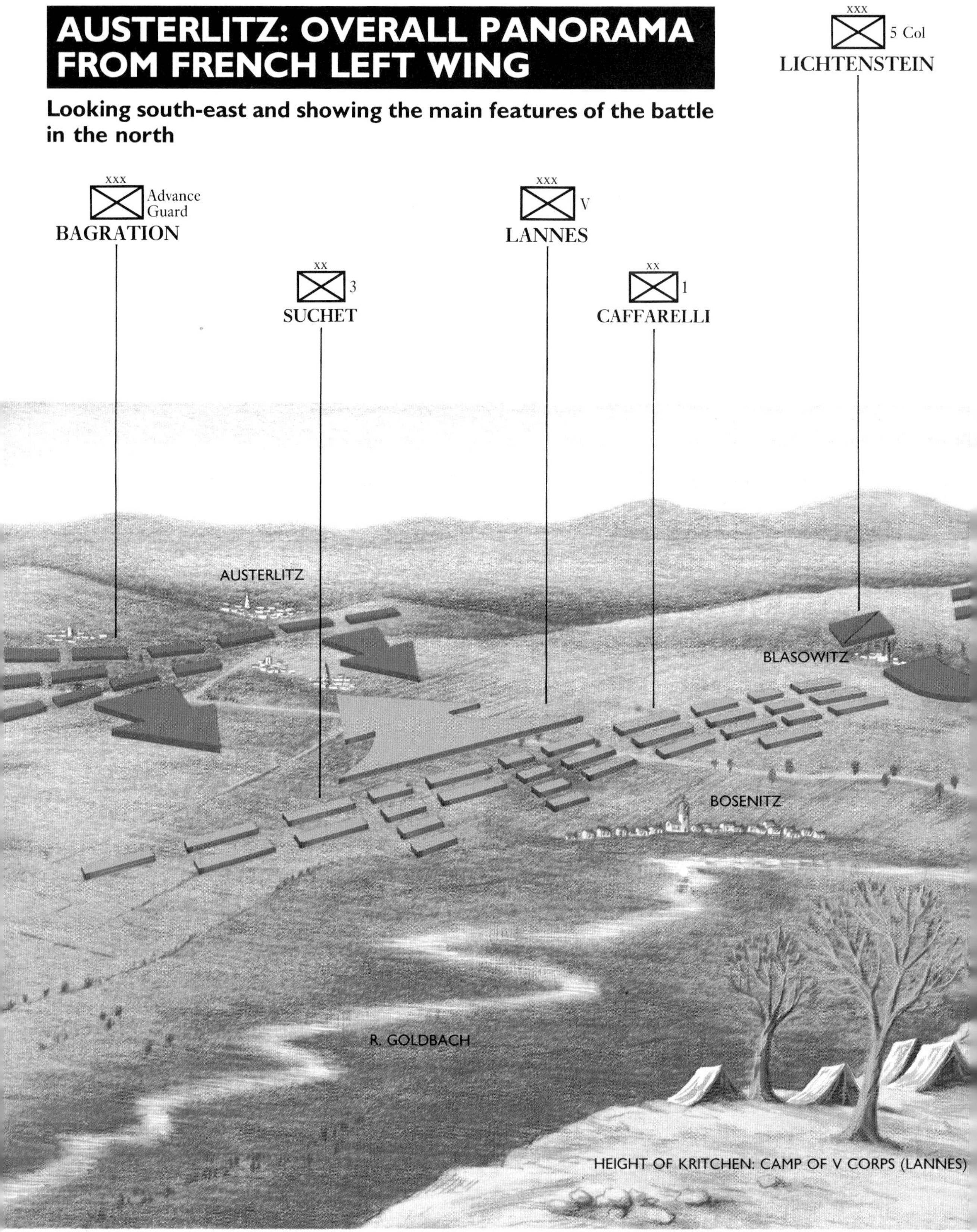

xxx
5 Col
LICHTENSTEIN

xxx
Advance Guard
BAGRATION

xxx
V
LANNES

xx
3
SUCHET

xx
1
CAFFARELLI

AUSTERLITZ

BLASOWITZ

BOSENITZ

R. GOLDBACH

HEIGHT OF KRITCHEN: CAMP OF V CORPS (LANNES)

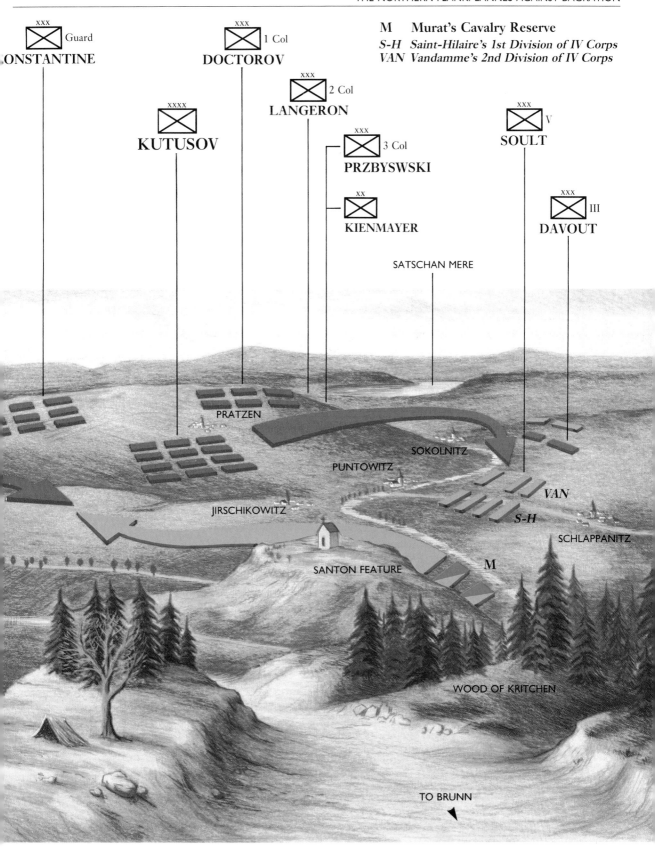

xxx
CONSTANTINE Guard

xxx
DOCTOROV 1 Col

xxx
LANGERON 2 Col

xxx
KUTUSOV

xxx
PRZBYSWSKI 3 Col

xx
KIENMAYER

xxx
SOULT V

xxx
DAVOUT III

M Murat's Cavalry Reserve
S-H *Saint-Hilaire's 1st Division of IV Corps*
VAN *Vandamme's 2nd Division of IV Corps*

SATSCHAN MERE

PRATZEN

SOKOLNITZ

PUNTOWITZ

VAN

JIRSCHIKOWITZ

S-H

SCHLAPPANITZ

SANTON FEATURE

M

WOOD OF KRITCHEN

TO BRUNN

(See also illustration on page 65 overleaf.)

the ultimate reserve – the Russian Imperial Guard.

On this part of the field Lichtenstein brought several batteries of horse and reserve artillery into action, striving to fill the developing gap between Bagration and the rest of the Allied army. He also lost no time in sending the Lothringen cuirassier regiment to strengthen the sparse Allied defences on Staré Vinohrady. At the same time the battalion of Russian Guard *Jaeger* was moving towards the village of Bläsowitz on Lichtenstein's left, supported by the cuirassier regiments of Nassau and Kaiser drawn up behind the village. In all, forty guns accompanied Bagration.

The action on this secondary battlefield opened with exchanges of artillery fire. Then Lichtenstein launched some 4,000 of his imposing cavalry in attacks against V Corps and its supporting horsemen. He found more than he bargained for: the close-range fire of Lannes's divisional 8pdr and regimental 4pdr cannon fired canister at point-blank range into the dense masses of manoeuvring horsemen, and this murderous hail was supplemented by French infantry volleys and cavalry carbine fire. The Austrian cavaliers flinched and drew back to be reformed by General Uvarov.

Prince John of Lichtenstein. Prince John was an Austrian lieutenant-general entrusted with the bulk of the Allied cavalry at Austerlitz, forming the fifth column, and was in fact the senior Austrian officer present after the

One Allied regiment, however, the Grand Duke Constantine's Uhlans, insisted on continuing their attack totally unsupported. Some of General Kellermann's light cavalry were scattered by this onslaught, but then the lancers rode on past the face of both Caffarelli's and Suchet's divisions, receiving blast after blast of musketry fire until all of 400 saddles – including that of General Essen, mortally wounded – were emptied and many horses brought down. The remnants of this brave but rash unit disappeared up the road towards Olmütz to be seen no more, leaving their colonel and 16 of their officers as French prisoners.

Kellermann took the opportunity to advance with his left-hand regiments, but this move provoked Lichtenstein to counter-charge. The French horsemen rode for cover, and when the Allied cavalry thundered up behind them towards Caffarelli's calmly-waiting ranks these 'opened up their intervals as cooly as if they had been on the parade ground. As soon as Kellermann's cavalry passed through they reformed their lines and opened fire on the enemy', according to one eye-witness on Napoleon's staff, General Thiard.

Back came Kellermann's squadrons – only to be fallen upon by the green-and-blue uniformed Pavlograd Hussars, together with the Tver and St Petersburg Dragoons. Prince Murat and his staff – behind Kellermann – were forced to draw their sabres to defend themselves, and the overall situation was only redressed by the intervention of Nansouty and his impressive heavy cavalry from central reserve. His carabineers were first into action, smashing into the foe with a crash that was heard throughout the battlefield. On the horsemen rode, supported by the 2nd and 3rd Cuirassiers, to assail the head of Lichtenstein's column of massed cavalry – and soon both the Elisabetgrad Hussars and Chernigov Dragoons were in full flight.

Emperor Francis. He fought mainly on the Allied right centre but was decisively defeated by Murat's cuirassiers in the late morning. (Anne S. K. Brown Military Collection, Brown University)

Whereupon Nansouty recalled his well-disciplined troopers to reform and rest behind Caffarelli's cheering infantry. Stung by the rout of his leading formations, Lichtenstein flung his next formations against Caffarelli's right wing – only to see them repulsed by volleys from the French, who had no time to form square. Nansouty then reappeared with his reordered squadrons to complete the discomfiture of the Allied cavalry. Thundering through the intervals in the infantry line in two columns, horsehair plumes tossing and breast-plates gleaming in the sun, the 'heavies' reformed into line and then charged, all seven regiments of them, into the stunned Allied ranks. Such pressure was not to be withstood, and very soon the hand-to-hand combat that ensued ended in the French favour.

It was now almost 10.30am. Lannes decided to exploit the discomfiture of Lichtenstein's squadrons by sending forward from Caffarelli's Division the *13ème Légére* and the 1st and 2nd Battalions of the *51ème Ligne* to attack the defenders of Bläsowitz. This village had been attacked by part of Bernadotte's I Corps earlier in the morning, but in the end without success. On this occasion, however, once again fortune smiled upon the French. Although the first French light infantry probe was sent back by the Guard *Jaeger*, the Russian troops immediately afterwards abandoned the village because they had become aware that French soldiers (part of Vandamme's Division in fact) were atop the Staré Vinohrady feature and a French battery was being established there. As the Guard light infantry drew back from this threat to their left and rear they found themselves assailed from the right as well by the 2nd Battalion of the *51ème*, who had worked their way round Bläsowitz. The Russians lost 500 prisoners and five guns in this incident.

As Lannes ordered his two infantry divisions to advance, they came under heavy and (for the young

Austerlitz, 10am, by Larbalestier. This fine panoramic view, sketched from a height near the town of Kritchen, shows (left) the divisions of Marshal Lannes' V Corps holding back Bagration's right wing, while beyond the chapel-topped Santon feature (foreground, right) *Soult's IV Corps storms the slopes of the Pratzen Heights. Meanwhile, to the south (far right) the battle rages as Buxhöwden's massive outflanking attack is held by Generals Legrand and Friant. (Anne S. K. Brown Military Collection, Brown University)*

French infantry repel Russian Cossacks, by Goupil. Bicorned French soldiers in desperate close action against the Tsar's light cavalry. Hand-to-hand fighting of this nature took place around Sokolnitz and Telnitz on the French right flank, where the brigade of Levasseur was beset by the Cossack regiments of Sysoev and Melentev. (Anne S. K. Brown Military Collection, Brown University)

conscripts) unsettling fire. Within three minutes 400 Frenchmen had been struck down, but ignoring the wounded as ordered the men marched on. Among the casualties was General Valhubert, his leg shattered by an exploding howitzer shell. 'Remember the Order of the Day,' he called out, 'Take no notice of me – only of the enemy. Close your ranks! If you come back as conquerors you can pick me up after the battle. If you are overcome, I have no desire for life!' (He in fact died of his wounds next day at Brünn.)

On the extreme northern flank, meantime, two battalions of the 5th *Jaeger* drove part of the *17ème Légère* out of some vineyards, and the pursuit was then taken up by the Mariupol Hussars and some Cossacks. The Russians reached Bosenitz, but then a strong counter-attack by the remainder of the *17ème* from the Santon drove the enemy back once more.

Midday – and Bagration's wing of the Allied army was evidently giving ground. On the northern flank, Treilhard and Milhaud led their light cavalry to force back the 5th *Jaeger* and Cossacks towards the Goldbach Heights. In the centre, Prince Murat – the very personification of courage and

determined dash – unleashed d'Hautpoul's cuirassiers in support of Kellermann and Walther, and a heavy cavalry engagement ensued near what had been Bagration's start-line, in which General Sébastiani was wounded. This action uncovered Bagration's right flank to cavalry attack and the Russian infantry halted and prepared to receive cavalry. However, soon after their horsemen came the panting infantrymen of Suchet's Division – an excellent example of combined tactics – who soon induced the Russians to recommence their retreat after losing some 2,000 casualties and 16 cannon. Many of the survivors also lost their personal possessions. As they advanced over the original Russian position the French *fantassins* came upon 10,000 knapsacks according to Lejeune, the famous war artist, all neatly laid out in straight rows. The troops fell upon this legitimate booty with whoops of glee – only to fling the packs down again in disappointment. 'All we got were 10,000 little black boxes of two-leaved reliquaries ... and 10,000 hunks of black bread, made of straw and bran rather than barley and wheat.' Some of the latter, however unappetizing, was wolfed down by the Frenchmen. Whatever their scorn for such rations, food of any type had been in short supply in the *Grande Armée*'s cantonments for several days.

One o'clock – and Bagration attempted to form a new line well past the posting inn where the road to Austerlitz forked off the Brünn to Olmütz highway. At this juncture he received a welcome reinforcement. The Austrian Major Frierenberger arrived from Olmütz at the head of a train of a dozen guns, which with commendable attention to his duty he managed to force through the fleeing crowds of Allied stragglers to site them on a low eminence north of the high road. Brought rapidly into action, their fire silenced several French regimental guns, and according to Austrian sources this earned a pause for the Allied right wing.

French sources claim that the halting of Suchet's division was deliberate rather than enforced. Marshal Lannes was becoming anxious lest V Corps' advance outstrip events in the centre of the battlefield, where indeed the last great climax of the day's fighting was taking place. Lannes had no wish to expose his own right flank to a possible counter-stroke from the south.

Although Bagration's wing was still in reasonable order, there could be no denying that it had suffered a defeat. The Allied right wing was now back behind the Raussnitz stream all of four miles east of the Santon. Estimates of losses vary, but at the very least the Russian right wing may be said to have suffered 2,500 killed and some 4,000 more taken prisoner. For the French, perhaps 2,000 casualties is reasonably near the mark.

The Russian Guard Intervenes: 'For God, the Tsar and Holy Russia'

While events were unfolding on the secondary battlefield on the northern flank, the centre of the Allied line was the scene of the most significant fighting of the day.

The tired but jubilant men of IV Corps stood masters of the Pratzen but the respite was to prove short-lived. The *10ème Légère* – on the extreme right of Saint-Hilaire's Division (which had occupied the village of Pratzen and secured the plateau in its vicinity after a stiff engagement with the Novgorod Regiment and the Little Russia Grenadiers) was suddenly attacked by Kaminsky's

French grenadier, showing typical campaign variation of uniform including long, loose trousers. (Philip J. Haythornthwaite)

returning part of the Second Column. It might well have been overwhelmed had not the divisional commander himself brought up a battalion of the *14ème Ligne* to its rescue at the double. Soon General Thiébault became aware of more formations to the east of his brigade. The fog of battle-smoke was intense at this moment, and the Austrians – for such they were – advanced, calling out that they were 'Bavarians, and friends'. Thiébault was too experienced a soldier to fall for such a ruse, and as a precaution deployed his whole brigade into a right-angled line, the apex being formed by the *36ème*, which was supported by the timely arrival of the Corps artillery from reserve: three 12pdrs being wheeled into position on each flank of the infantry regiment. Soon all doubts were dispelled when an officer from Kaminsky's column was seen to run over and consult with a 'Bavarian' officer. Double-shotting the 12pdrs with a round of canister on top of all, the French gunners waited, crouched around their pieces. The newcomers were allowed to get within 150 yards of the French line before the order to fire was given. The gunners pressed their glowing linstocks to the touch-holes, and with a cavernous roar the 12pdrs leapt up and back as they discharged their death-dealing salvoes. Gaps were torn in the approaching formations. Soon musketry volleys added to the din.

Although the Austrian units concerned were far from élite, they fought with desperation, aided by Weyrother and his staff and under the eye of Kutusov and the Tsar in person. For 30 minutes the struggle swayed to and fro, each side losing severe casualties. At one point Saint-Hilaire considered withdrawal, but was dissuaded by Colonel Pousedt of the *10ème Légère* – who pointed out that his men, again under attack from the south, could only hold where they stood. The scene was piled with bodies before the Austrians pulled back.

But help was at hand. General Langeron arrived in person at the head of two battalions of the Kursk Regiment backed by the Podolia Regiment just as Kaminsky's men broke. Langeron found himself attacked frontally by Thiébault's survivors and taken in flank by General Levasseur's brigade – part of General Legrand's 3rd Division, which was sufficiently in command of the fighting in the Goldbach valley to be able to spare this formation – which had just reached the heights. The Kursk Regiment was decimated – losing some 1,550 men, its regimental guns and, worst of all, its colours. The Podolia Regiment soon found itself going down the hill ever faster, taking Langeron with it,

and only halted when it reached the stone wall of the Sokolnitz pheasantry. Langeron at once went to report to General Buxhöwden, sitting with his staff nearby. The commander of the Allied left wing refused to credit Langeron's tidings. 'My dear general,' he brusquely informed Langeron, 'you seem to see the foe everywhere.' 'And you, Count, are in no state to see the enemy anywhere!' snapped his subordinate. Allied tempers were becoming decidedly frayed.

Meanwhile Vandamme was in firm possession of the Staré Vinohrady feature, having also deployed his three brigades into line so as to achieve maximum fire potential. It had required a full-scale frontal assault to dislodge the Salzburg Regiment from the peak. His second brigade pressed Kollowrath's troops back towards Krzenowitz, and it was clear that the Russian Fourth Column had shot its bolt. During this stage of the fighting the Tsar had been covered by flying earth from a near miss and was persuaded to withdraw his august person. General Kutusov received a slight wound to the head amid the din and confusion and only received treatment at Hostieradek at the eastern foot of the Pratzen, having accompanied Kaminsky's shattered regiments thither. These events assured the French of control of the Pratzen – but, despite appearances, the battle was by no means yet over.

Over on the Zurlan, Napoleon had been kept in touch with developments by his semaphore station and the arrival of mounted messengers. Certain

Pratzen village as it is today, viewed from Telnitz. (Author's Collection)

that the battle on each flank was proceeding satisfactorily, about midday he decided to transfer his command post to the highest point of the Pratzen, ordering a general advance by the Imperial Guard, Oudinot's Grenadiers and the whole of Bernadotte's I Corps in the same general direction. The Music of the Guard struck up *'On va leur percer le flanc'* and the élite moved impressively forwards 'in full parade uniform with bearskin caps and plumes flying in the wind, and uncased eagle-standards and pennants' as Guardsman Barrès recalled, and 'climbed the far Heights to cries of *Vive l'Empereur!*' In due course Napoleon and his staff repositioned themselves on Staré Vinohrady. The Emperor had still not made up his mind whether to envelop the northern or the southern wing of the Allied army. 'One engages, then one sees.' As always, he was capable of adjusting his intentions to suit prevailing circumstances: he was the past-master of the alternate plan.

Reining in his horse near the summit Napoleon found a panorama of conflict spread out below him. The sky had clouded over, but visibility remained good. He arrived in the nick of time to observe the Allied last throw of the dice – for looking to the east there was no missing the impressive approach of the Grand Duke Constantine and the Russian Imperial Guard Corps.

This august formation had not had an entirely uneventful morning. The Guard *Jaeger* battalion had been sent to occupy Bläswitz, supported by a battalion of the Semenovsky Lifeguard Regiment – but only to be forced to retire from the village as has already been described. A message from the Tsar next caused Constantine to detach a battalion of the Ismailovsky Life Guards to assist in the fighting on the Pratzen plateau, but it arrived only in time to see, and participate in, the total repulse of Miloradovich and Kollowrath. This untoward event caused Constantine to withdraw the Guard Corps behind the Raussnitz tributary at 11.30am, hoping there to rally the remnants of the shaken Fourth Column. This move was covered by artillery and a light infantry screen, and it eased the pressure on General Hohenlohe's force of Austrian cuirassiers who were able to disengage from the environs of Bläswitz and retire to Krzenowitz before reforming on the rearward flanks of the

The Grand Duke Constantine. Constantine (1779–1831) was the younger brother of the Tsar, whom he served in many capacities. He was praised for his handling of the Russian Imperial Guard Corps at Austerlitz, but his strong counter-attack up the eastern slopes of the Pratzen Heights came too late to affect the outcome of the battle. Arguably, his attack was launched from too far to the rear. (Anne S. K. Brown Military Collection, Brown University)

Russian Guard. But soon the Guard Corps found itself under fire from Vandamme's divisional artillery, newly deployed upon the summit of Staré Vinohrady. Once again the Archduke felt compelled to order yet another demonstration of force – this time a major one consisting of the élite Semenovsky and Preobrazhensky Grenadier Regiments, covered by the Guard *Jaeger*, and with the Guard cavalry on each flank. This force was ordered to occupy the eastern end of the Staré Vinohrady.

Hardly had this manoeuvre begun than the Guardsmen found themselves under attack by General Schinner's 3rd Brigade of Vandamme's Division, which was advancing along the northern slopes of the feature under dispute. This complication forced the Archduke to order an all-out attack instead of a demonstration in strength. It was shortly after 1pm as Ferdinand led up these

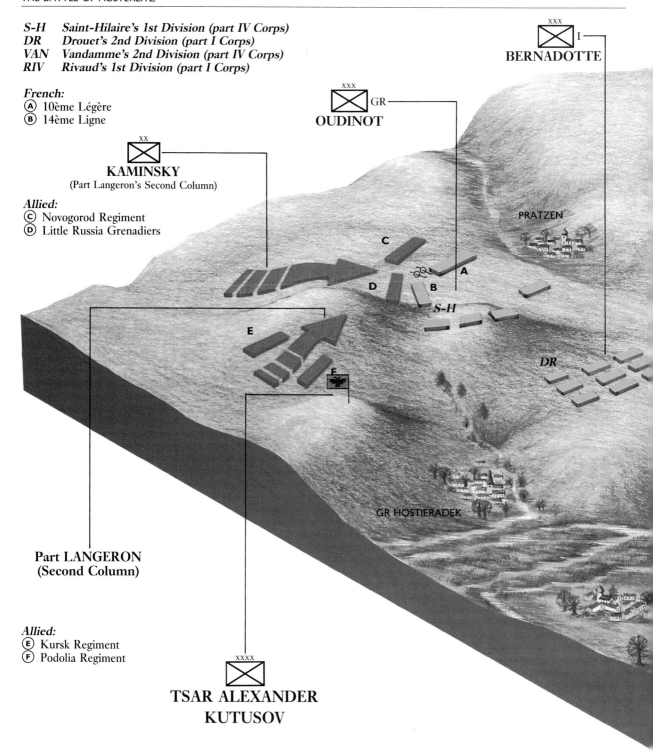

S-H *Saint-Hilaire's 1st Division (part IV Corps)*
DR *Drouet's 2nd Division (part I Corps)*
VAN *Vandamme's 2nd Division (part IV Corps)*
RIV *Rivaud's 1st Division (part I Corps)*

French:
Ⓐ 10ème Légère
Ⓑ 14ème Ligne

KAMINSKY
(Part Langeron's Second Column)

Allied:
Ⓒ Novogorod Regiment
Ⓓ Little Russia Grenadiers

OUDINOT GR

BERNADOTTE I

PRATZEN

S-H

DR

GR HOSTIERADEK

Part LANGERON
(Second Column)

Allied:
Ⓔ Kursk Regiment
Ⓕ Podolia Regiment

TSAR ALEXANDER
KUTUSOV

COUNTER-ATTACK OF
THE RUSSIAN IMPERIAL GUARD

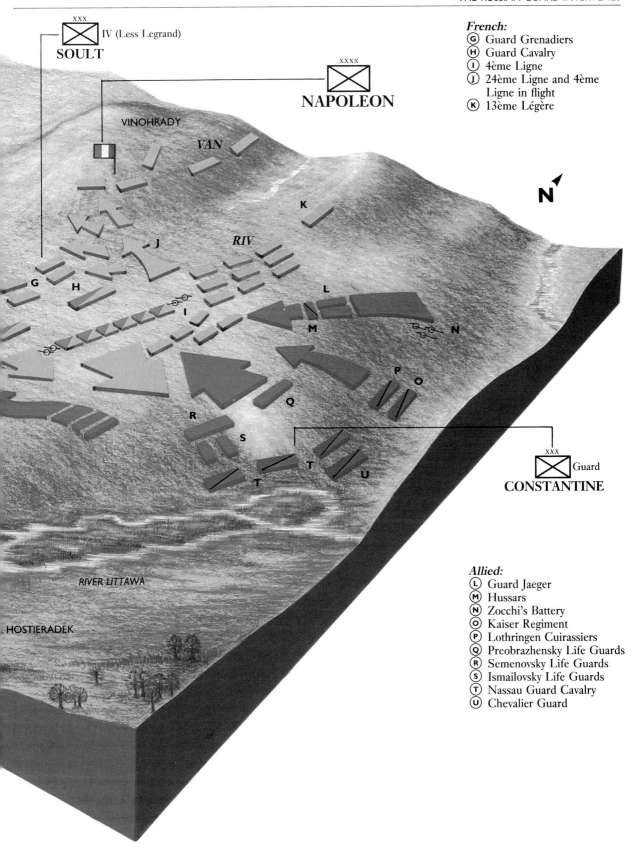

XXX

SOULT
IV (Less Legrand)

XXXX

NAPOLEON

VINOHRADY

VAN

N

K

RIV

J

G

H

I

L

M

N

P

O

Q

R

S

T

T

U

XXX
Guard
CONSTANTINE

RIVER LITTAWA

HOSTIERADEK

French:
- **G** Guard Grenadiers
- **H** Guard Cavalry
- **I** 4ème Ligne
- **J** 24ème Ligne and 4ème Ligne in flight
- **K** 13ème Légère

Allied:
- **L** Guard Jaeger
- **M** Hussars
- **N** Zocchi's Battery
- **O** Kaiser Regiment
- **P** Lothringen Cuirassiers
- **Q** Preobrazhensky Life Guards
- **R** Semenovsky Life Guards
- **S** Ismailovsky Life Guards
- **T** Nassau Guard Cavalry
- **U** Chevalier Guard

71

élite battalions, totalling some 3,000 Grenadiers. Unfortunately the control of the advance slipped, and with 300 yards still to go the Grenadiers broke into a run, so that by the time they reached their objective most of the men were seriously out of breath. This notwithstanding, the brass-mitred giants broke through the first French line – only to be brought to a halt in front of the second by a hurricane of French artillery fire. The Guard then retired to reform near Krzenowitz in excellent order.

Napoleon was a witness to these developments and sent an aide to Vandamme with an order to incline to his right to increase pressure on the reforming Russian Guardsmen. Vandamme ordered the move to be made – but in doing so uncovered his left flank and rear. Such an opportunity did not go unnoticed by the Archduke, who immediately ordered the 15 available squadrons of the Guard cavalry, led by 1,000 cuirassiers, to destroy Vandamme from the flank while the Grenadiers returned to the attack from the front. In the nick of time the *4ème Ligne's* foremost battalion formed square on Major Bigarré's order. But the Russian cavalry swung aside to reveal six horse-artillery pieces trained on the square, which received a hail of death-dealing canister. Vandamme, already wounded earlier in the fray, rushed the *24ème Légère* to the *4ème's* rescue, but it could not make its presence felt

before the cuirassiers fell upon the battered square with immense shock. Over 200 French infantry were cut down, and the *4ème's* treasured eagle-standard was captured, to be borne off in triumph to the rear. Aghast the *24ème Léger* decided to deploy rather than share the fate of their comrades' square – but the mass of Russian Guard cavalry broke over and through them in a thundering wave of shouting men and snorting horses. The survivors of the *24ème* thereupon joined those of the *4ème* in a flight towards the rear of their army, leaving many French dead amongst the vine stumps.

The Emperor was astounded to see this tide of humanity rushing towards him. At first his staff optimistically declared them to be Russian prisoners, but they were soon disabused on this score. Napoleon's staff rode forward to attempt to rally the fugitives who at one moment threatened to overrun the Emperor in person. 'Our attempts to arrest it [the *4ème Ligne*] were all in vain,' recorded de Ségur. 'The unfortunate fellows were quite distracted with fear and would listen to no one; in reply to our reproaches for thus deserting the field

Austerlitz, by Dupleissis-Berbaux. Note the artillerie volante ('flying artillery') middle-ground right. These light guns were expected to be capable of keeping up with cavalry and in *consequence all their gunners were mounted on horseback rather than perched upon the ammunition caissons. (Anne S. K. Brown Military Collection, Brown University)*

of battle and their Emperor they shouted mechanically "*Vive l'Empereur*" while fleeing faster than ever.' Despite the gravity of the moment even Napoleon was noticed to smile at this ludicrous situation. 'Let them go,' he ordered.

The gap in Vandamme's line clearly needed attention without delay. He turned to Marshal Bessières, commander of the Imperial Guard. He in turn signalled to Colonel Morland, who at once advanced at the head of two squadrons of *chasseurs-à-cheval* supported by three of the *grosse-bottes* ('the big-boots') or *grenadiers-à-cheval* under General Ordener and a further squadron of *chasseurs* accompanied by a battery of horse artillery. A confused mêlée ensued, each side taking heavy casualties amidst the vineyards – but then Constantine sent in his remaining cavalry – namely the *Chevalier Gardes* (recruited from only the noblest families in Russia) and the Guard Cossacks. The French Guard cavalry found themselves assailed on three sides – not least by the towering Semenovsky and Preobrazjensky Life Guards, who were now back deep in the fray. Morland fell dead. It required *les grosse-bottes* aided by the unlimbered horse artillery to extricate the decimated *chasseurs*.

The situation looked grave. But now on to the scene marched Drouet d'Erlon's leading brigade of I Corps under Colonel Gérard, diverted from its original mission to reinforce Saint-Hilaire – at Marshal Soult's suggestion, on Bernadotte's initiative (according to the Gascon Marshal) or on receipt of a direct order from Napoleon (according to the Emperor). The newcomers earned the French a slight respite, during which Napoleon summoned his senior aide-de-camp, General Jean Rapp, and told him to lead more Guard cavalry into the maelstrom. At the head of the ferocious squadron of 250 Mamelukes of the Guard and two more of *chasseurs-à-cheval*, Rapp swept forward in his turn. The Mamelukes in their sumptuous oriental robes (although many of them were Frenchmen) made a frightening sight, and the horses fought as viciously as their riders. The *chasseurs* proved rather less successful, until Napoleon ordered to their support a squadron of *grenadiers-à-cheval*. For fifteen minutes the action surged and eddied amid an immense cloud of

Jean Baptiste Drouet d'Erlon, Commander of the 2nd Division in Marshal Bernadotte's I Corps at Austerlitz, Drouet (1765–1844) was a distinguished general officer of the Napoleonic Wars, who was made Comte d'Erlon in 1809.

After Waterloo (where he commanded I Corps) he fled abroad but was pardonned by King Charles X in 1825, and in 1843 he was appointed a Marshal of France. (Anne S. K. Brown Military Collection, Brown University)

powder smoke and dust, causing the Foot Grenadiers of the Imperial Guard to feel their way forward with caution lest they attack their own compatriots. Drouet d'Erlon's brigade repelled a bold Russian attempt to ride through their intervals and engage the rallying *chasseurs* beyond.

In the press the Russian Guardsmen could not fire their muskets for fear of hitting the Chevalier Guard, who were taking appalling casualties from the long swords of the *grenadiers-à-cheval*. Then suddenly it was over. The Russian Imperial Guard retraced its steps towards Krzenowitz, covered by Austrian cuirassiers. Had Bernadotte pressed ahead with the rest of his troops, few Guardsmen would have escaped, but the commander of I Corps preferred to halt his men on the edge of the heights overlooking the village.

Charge of the Mamelukes, after Myrbach. Since his expedition to Egypt in 1798–9, part of Napoleon's escort had consisted of colourfully-dressed Mamelukes (whose inspiration had been the mounted warriors of Murad and Ibrahim Bey). At Austerlitz they took part in General Jean Rapp's charge against the Russian Imperial Guard, which clinched the battle on the Pratzen Heights. (Author's Collection)

General Rapp, slightly wounded, rode up to the Emperor to report on his success and to present the disconsolate stream of some 200 disarmed Chevalier Guards being herded back as prisoners, who included Prince Repnine, their commander. 'Many fine ladies of St Petersburg will lament this day,' commented Napoleon. Next to arrive on the scene was Mustapha (a genuine Mameluke from Egyptian days in 1798). He bore a captured standard, which he disdainfully laid at his master's feet, exclaiming, 'If me catch Constantine, me cut off his head and me bring to Emperor!' He had only been deprived of his prey because the Archduke had managed to wound Mustapha's steed with a lucky pistol shot.

It was shortly after two o'clock. The Russian centre had now effectively ceased to exist, and Napoleon was poised to deliver the *coup de grâce*. The heavy fighting on the Pratzen Heights and around Staré Vinohrady had not gone exactly as Napoleon had foreseen, but his ability to extemporize solutions to new situations had been amply demonstrated, and there was no denying that he had secured the grand tactical objective that he had set his sights on from the first – namely the occupation of the Allied centre. All around him lay the still corpses of the dead of three nations, all entangled and interspersed with the groaning and twitching wounded whom the surgeons now came forward to aid. The Frenchmen noted with awe

how philosophical were the Russian peasant-soldiers among the wounded: however gravely injured, hardly a sound escaped then.

Victory was now assured for the French; but it still remained to convert it into total triumph.

The Fate of General Buxhöwden

Napoleon carefully examined the field through his telescope. One last major decision had to be taken, involving another adjustment to the original plan. By this, despite what the doctored Order of the Day would lead us to believe, he had envisaged enveloping Bagration's wing of the Allied army after the capture of the Pratzen Heights. But Bagration, although repulsed, still had his men in good order and had taken up a position rather too far to the east for the convenience of the French. So the Emperor decided to wheel the French centre to its right, and set about the destruction of Buxhöwden's over-sized left wing, still fighting doggedly in the valley of the Goldbach against Legrand and Davout. The newly disclosed aim therefore was to take in rear the three Allied columns still in being.

Accordingly Bernadotte was ordered to secure the Pratzen and Staré Vinohrady with his still relatively fresh I Corps, while Saint-Hilaire and Vandamme, followed by the Imperial Guard, swung to the south.

Soon everything was in motion. Saint-Hilaire's First Division, with General Férey's brigade of Vandamme's Second, moved off on the right and began to descend from the Pratzen Heights towards Sokolnitz, while Levasseur's brigade of General Legrand's hard-fighting command emerged from the Sokolnitz area to form on Saint-Hilaire's right, followed by the divisional commander in person at the head of General Merle's Brigade to take post on Saint-Hilaire's left. Boyé's Dragoon Division closed up behind Vandamme, whose remaining two brigades marched south to line up along the cliffs forming the southern extremity of the plateau, from which they would threaten Buxhöwden's line of retreat. In support of all marched the Imperial Guard with Napoleon at its head.

All this time Marshal Davout and General Friant had been fighting doggedly around the west and south of Sokolnitz, pinning down the greater part of Langeron's and Przbyswski's Columns. With consummate timing, Friant now launched a full-scale attack, using the *33ème Ligne* to assault the western edge of Sokolnitz while what remained of the *48ème Ligne*, accompanied by the surviving *Tirailleurs du Pô* and *Corses*, stormed into the southern outskirts of the village and penetrated as far as the castle. The streets of the town were carpeted with French and Allied dead and wounded – truly an appalling sight.

The Battle of Austerlitz, after Gérard. This well-known picture shows General Rapp, who had led the charge of the Guard cavalry against the Russian Grand Duke Constantine's Guard Corps at the crisis on the Pratzen, presenting prisoners of the Chevalier Guard (including their commander, Prince Repnine) and captured standards to the Emperor. (Anne S. K. Brown Military Collection, Brown University)

This new attack came at the worst possible moment for the Allies who were just becoming aware of French troops beginning to occupy the overlooking cliffs at the southern end of the Pratzen feature. Furthermore, they were also called upon to meet Saint-Hilaire's reinforced columns – which were soon attacking the walls around the park of the pheasantry near Sokolnitz. The *36ème Ligne* was led off by General Thiébault to take part in General Friant's attack on Sokolnitz Castle, while Levasseur's regiments headed for the ground linking the park to the village.

Only a single thought now motivated the Allied column commanders (the high command had long-since ceased to operate effectively): retreat. This they attempted to do in several directions. General Langeron led off the 8th *Jaeger* and the Viborg Regiment due south, and in due course made good his escape from the field. A second group was less fortunate: the Perm Musketeers and much of the 7th *Jaeger* were forced away north-west and isolated from the rest of Buxhöwden's wing. Part of these

troops tried to hold Sokolnitz Castle and its out buildings, defending every byre and cottage with frenzied determination, but in the end being flushed out on to higher ground beyond the castle. At this point General Thiébault was wounded in the shoulder. A third force, the Galician and Butyrsk Regiments, together with parts of the Narva, Azov and Podolia Regiments, under the personal command of Generals Przbyswsky, Selekov and Strik, attempted to break out to the north towards Kobelnitz, where they hoped to discover the Fourth Column (which in fact was over two miles away in full retreat to the east). Przbyswsky soon found himself under attack from three directions at once – his rear by the *36ème Ligne*, his left by part of Oudinot's Grenadier Division, and the right by both Morand and Levasseur. Losing men every yard, this battered

Austerlitz, after Muller. Another representation of the later stages of the great battle. Watched by the Imperial Guard (left foreground) and the Horse Grenadiers of the Guard (left middle-ground), Napoleon coordinates the movements needed to complete the discomfiture of the Tsar's and Austrian Emperor's armies. (Anne S. K. Brown Military Collection, Brown University)

force eventually found itself trapped against the frozen Sokolnitz mere or pond. The *36ème* surged forward towards Przbysewsky crying 'Prisoner! Prisoner!', but were forestalled by a party of the *8ème Hussards* under Colonel Franceschi-Delonne to the fury of General Lochet. Although some devoted Russian NCOs tried to hide their regimental colours by stripping them from their poles and placing them under their uniforms, all of 4,000 men were obliged to surrender.

Napoleon and his Staff at Austerlitz, after Myrbach. The scene shows the Emperor outside the Chapel of St Anthony after the heights of Pratzen had been stormed by Generals Saint-Hilaire and Vandamme of Marshal Soult's IV Corps. Note the officer in the foreground wearing the brassard of a staff officer on his left arm. In the distance, French reinforcements, including the Imperial Guard, toil up the slopes to secure the captured position in the Allied centre. (Author's Collection)

On all sides order and discipline were breaking down. Small parties of the Allies continued to fight on, but there was no longer any synchronization. The Austrian Lieutenant-General Wimpfen was the next to be forced to surrender with a detachment of the Narva Regiment.

What was left of Doctorov's, Kienmayer's and Langeron's commands found themselves cut off to the south of Sokolnitz – assailed by Boyé's *3ème Division de Dragons* and Vandamme's infantry on the one side, and Friant's men of III Corps and Saint-Hilaire's brigades from the west and north respectively. The ice-cold Davout had given the grim order, 'No prisoners!' and there was much bayonet-work amongst the helpless Russian and Austrian wounded.

Napoleon and his staff had now reached the Chapel of St Anthony on the southern slopes of the Pratzen and there was joined by Marshal Soult and General Vandamme. Pointing down at the village of Aujest Markt below – which afforded the only practicable Allied line of retreat – the Emperor ordered Vandamme to seize it without delay. Already thousands of Allied troops were pouring away over the plain and past – and in many cases over – the frozen Satschan and Menitz meres. But Vandamme's units were only appearing little by little, and a large Russian battery (some sources say of as many as 50 guns, although this is doubtful) was sweeping the lower slopes with concentrated fire, so it was a little time before this could be effected. The French had 25 cannon limbered up and approaching from the north, but on the way they found themselves attacked by some wandering Austrian dragoons, which caused a further delay. At last a battalion of the *28ème Ligne* forced its way

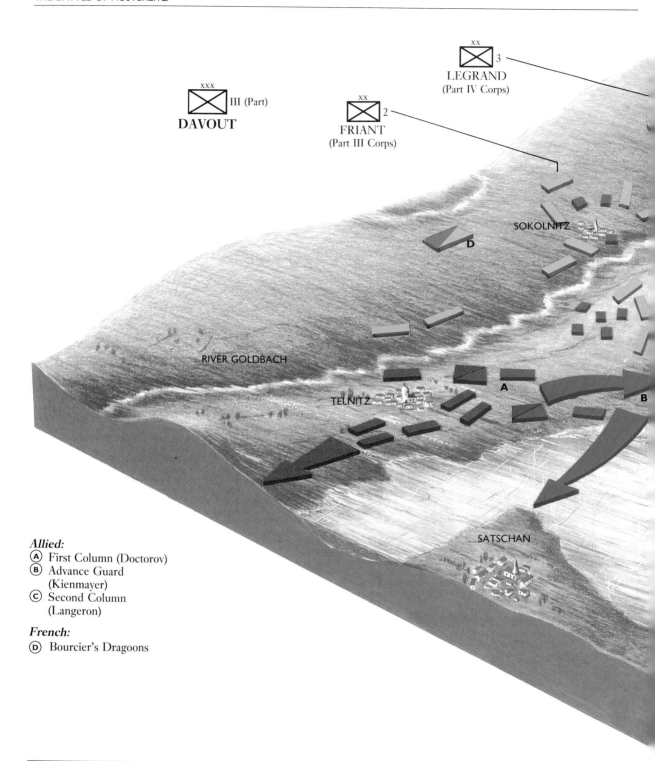

XXX

III (Part)

DAVOUT

XX

2

FRIANT
(Part III Corps)

XX

3

LEGRAND
(Part IV Corps)

SOKOLNITZ

D

RIVER GOLDBACH

TELNITZ

A

B

SATSCHAN

Allied:
Ⓐ First Column (Doctorov)
Ⓑ Advance Guard
   (Kienmayer)
Ⓒ Second Column
   (Langeron)

French:
Ⓓ Bourcier's Dragoons

THE FLIGHT OF BUXHOWDEN'S WING OF THE AUSTRO-RUSSIAN ARMY

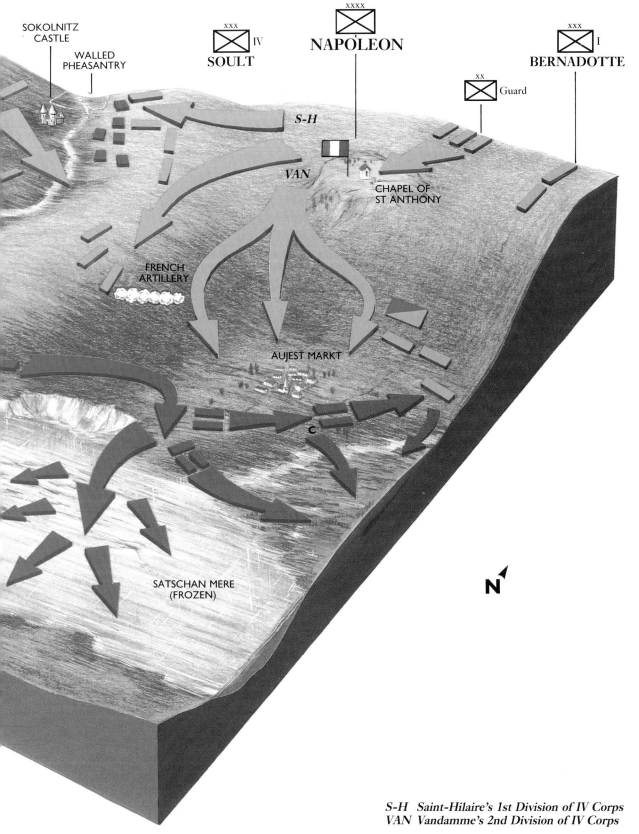

SOKOLNITZ
CASTLE

WALLED
PHEASANTRY

xxx
IV
SOULT

xxxx
NAPOLEON

xxx
I
BERNADOTTE

xx
Guard

S-H

VAN

CHAPEL OF
ST ANTHONY

FRENCH
ARTILLERY

AUJEST MARKT

c

SATSCHAN MERE
(FROZEN)

N

S-H Saint-Hilaire's 1st Division of IV Corps
VAN Vandamme's 2nd Division of IV Corps

to the east of Aujest Markt, severing the key road to Hostieradek and distant Austerlitz. At length the *24ème Léger*, the *4ème Ligne* and the rest of the *28ème* advanced past the chapel and forced their way down to the village. After a brief but sharp fight it was taken, and the 8th *Jaeger* with its colonel was rounded up. The Russian guns continued to fire until the very last moment, but then were overwhelmed. French casualties had been far from light. As Vandamme cryptically remarked (anticipating Karl von Clausewitz, the famous Prussian author of *On War* twenty years later), 'You cannot make omelettes without breaking eggs!'

Now – their best line of retreat severed – total disaster threatened the Allied left wing formations that still remained in the field. Here and there deeds of great valour were performed. A small force of Austrian cavalry and Russian Cossacks, together with a handful of infantry of both nations, clung on grimly near Telnitz trying to cover the retreat of the what was left of the Advance Guard and the First Column. Commanded in person by Generals Kienmayer and Doctorov, they began a fighting retreat towards the frozen ponds, abandoning Telnitz in the process. Three battalions at Satschan covered the road towards Aujest Markt together

with the Hessen-Homburg Hussars to the east, and Major-General Moritz Lichtenstein formed the rearguard with O'Reilly's *Chevaulégers*, a battery of horse artillery and some Cossacks.

Napoleon expected the *coup de grâce* to be administered by General Boyér's 3rd Division of Dragoons. That officer, however, unexpectedly dragged his feet, and the best opportunity passed. Napoleon was furious, and sent General of Brigade Charles-Mathieu Gardanne – Governor of the Pages in the Imperial Household – to take over command of the formation and charge forthwith. This attack, through the gathering dusk of a winter evening, did not go well – for some 15 Russian cannon commanded by Colonel Sievers suddenly revealed their presence with a thunderous salvo at close range, emptying many saddles. But the same fate was accorded to an attempted Austrian cavalry counter-attack led by Colonel O'Reilly, which ran straight into a deployed battery of the Guard Horse Artillery, to be decimated in its turn. A number of prisoners from the Austrian *Chevaulégers* fell into French hands.

Nevertheless, there was no disguising that a substantial part of the Allied left wing had made good its escape towards Austerlitz. Buxhöwden still

Battle of Austerlitz: the flight of the Russian army over the lakes, by Martiant. A somewhat fanciful representation of the last dramatic act of the battle. The town to the left is probably Satschan, while away in the distance to the right is the Chapel of St Anthony, the site of Napoleon's last battle headquarters on 2 December near the southern edge of the Pratzen Heights.

had many men to extricate. Any idea of getting more out through Aujest Markt was now out of the question as the French firmly sealed off that escape route. So Buxhöwden decided on a gamble – and headed for the single wooden bridge over the Littawa stream to the south of Aujest Markt. Leading the way, he and his staff passed over safely, but the first gun-team following behind smashed through the bridge and blocked it irretrievably. Without waiting for orders, the following infantry set out over the ice of the Satschan Pond – following on the heels of many individual fugitives who had preceded them over the slippery surface.

Allied gunner officers – denied the Littawa bridge – tried to use a narrow causeway dividing two parts of the mere. French artillery divulged their intention, and a well-placed – or just lucky – howitzer shell struck an ammunition wagon as it crossed the narrow way. A thunderous explosion rent the darkening evening air, and another escape route was blocked. A tail-back of immovable gun-teams inexorably developed behind the jam, while several managed to swerve gingerly on to the ice – and it appeared that it was strong enough to take their weight. However, according to the French account, Napoleon (the gunner) was not going to allow his prey to escape in this fashion, and ordered his artillery to fire deliberately to break it around the fugitives.

A desperate scene is conjured up of plunging cannon balls smashing and cracking the ice causing Allied men, horses and cannon to fall through to drown or die of exposure in the freezing water. The 30th Bulletin of the *Grande Armée* claimed that all of 20,000 Allies were thus destroyed. This is certainly a legend – or rather a deliberate falsification of the truth. Not for nothing did the catch-phrase '*mentir comme un bulletin*' ('to lie like a Bulletin') come into common use during the Napoleonic period. For one thing, most of the ponds of Satschan and Menitz to the south were too shallow to drown a man – although exhausted soldiers, many still encumbered with part or in some cases all of their arms and equipment, might well have died of shock or panic in the chaotic

Austerlitz – the last act, after Myrbach. As Buxhöwden's left wing attempted to escape over the frozen Satschan meres, Napoleon ordered up 25 guns to the southern edge of the overlooking Pratzen Heights and instructed them to break the ice. Perhaps 2,000 Allied soldiers and 38 gun-teams perished in the freezing waters. (Author's Collection)

Austerlitz: Situation 14.30 2 December 1805

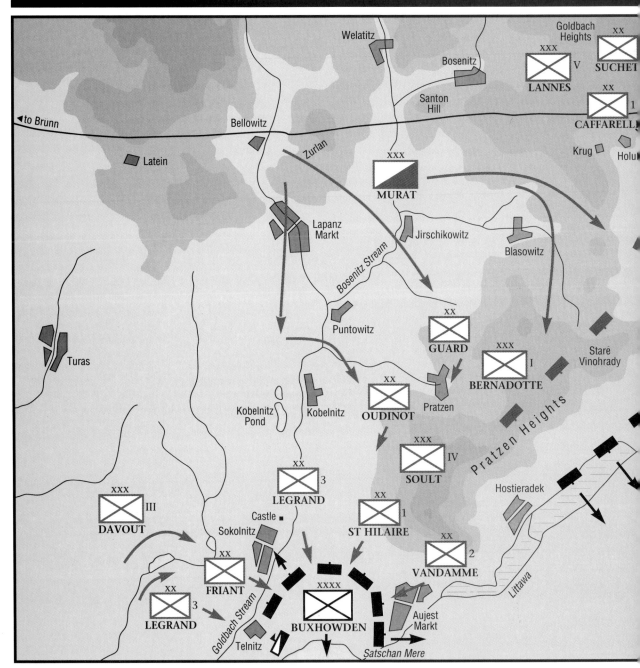

situation developing around them, as every man tried to save himself at the expense of no matter who else. However, the legend that dozens of Russian gun-teams crashed through the ice to their doom has been convincingly challenged. For one thing, only 5,000 Allied troops were in the area of the meres at this time. For another, it is known that

only 38 guns and 130 corpses of horses were recovered from the shallow lakes after the battle. At most, then, 2,000 men may have died; but some respected authorities put the number as only 200 drowned.

Many more Russians and Austrians were rounded up by the exhausted but jubilant French

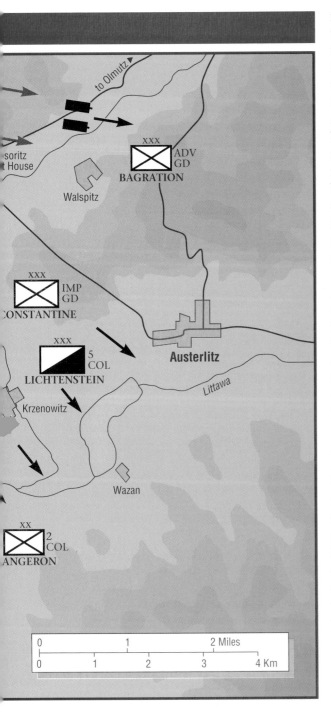

not one escape.' But now, as the sun settled below the horizon and snow began to fall, it was possible to exercise more mercy. By half past four the last firing had died away. Napoleon slowly rode down to the plain, Berthier, Soult and Bessières at his side. Cheers of '*Vive l'Empereur!*' greeted his appearance. An immense victory had been won, proving the battle-worthiness of the French army – probably the best Napoleon ever commanded – and the military genius of its chief. But the cost had not been light: over 9,000 French casualties (12 per cent) lay dead, dying or wracked with pain on the freezing ground. As the Duke of Wellington was to remark after Waterloo, 'Nothing but a battle lost is more terrible than a battle won.'

As was to be expected, the condition of the Allied army that had entered battle so confidently that same morning was far worse. As the bedraggled columns drew off in the gloom they left behind them 27,000 of their comrades (or 32 per cent), perhaps 12,000 of them prisoners of war, besides some 180 cannon. Bagration's wing drawn up at Raussnitz was in better condition, but he soon headed for Austerlitz town when he heard that the Allies were to retreat to Hungary. Lichtenstein's remaining cavalry and the Russian Imperial Guard – together with the Imperial suites and baggage – blocked the town and its immediate environs. As a result Kutusov, Kaminsky and Kollowrath, followed by Buxhöwden, had to lead their dispirited and dead-weary men (the last-named commander had barely 2,000 men with him – a mere 6 per cent of his original command) round Austerlitz to the south as they plodded their way eastwards. The village of Czitsch was designated for the rallying point of the army. The Tsar had become separated not only from his army but also from his staff; accompanied only by a surgeon and, eventually, Major Toll, he eventually found shelter seven miles from the battlefield at the village of Urchitz.

There was no pursuit. The victors were as exhausted as the vanquished. The French occupied their enemy's morning ground and enjoyed what sleep they could amid the snow, which spat and sizzled on the embers of the extemporized camp fires. Some went looking for friends among the wounded, and the surgeons began to ply their grisly trade beneath smoking lanterns. But there was no

soldiers. Up to this point very few prisoners had been taken. General Thiébault recorded that, 'Up to the last hour of the battle we took no prisoners, it would just not do to take any risk; one could stick at nothing, and thus not a single living enemy remained to our rear.' As with IV Corps, so with III Corps. Davout's simple order to his men was, 'Let

The Great Battle of Austerlitz, after Rugender. An imaginative overview of the battlefield with the town of *Austerlitz on the far horizon (centre). (Anne S. K. Brown Military Collection, Brown University)*

denying that the French soldiers were tough customers. The men of the *26ème Légère* of Legrand's 1st Brigade, for instance, were determined that their admired commander, Colonel Pouget, should enjoy a comfortable night. So, as that officer later recalled in his memoirs, 'they dragged together a number of Russian corpses, and spread a layer of hay on top'.

Napoleon slowly wended his way to the Posoritz post-house at the Austerlitz fork of the Brünn to Olmütz highway. En route, he continually paused to order aid to be given to wounded men, sometimes giving them brandy with his own hand. While his escort stripped off greatcoats from the Russian dead to lay over the wounded, Napoleon ate a simple supper, made up of army rations, and dried himself before a large fire. At midnight (some other sources claim it was just before dawn) the Austrian Prince Lichtenstein presented himself under a flag of truce and arranged a preliminary meeting between Napoleon and Francis II for the early afternoon of the 4th, to be held where the road

to Hungary crossed the Spálény rivulet. The Prince having left, the Emperor settled down to dictate his victory message to the army. He got as far as '*Soldats, Je suis content de vous . . .*' when weariness intervened. Before giving way to it he scribbled a short note to Josephine. 'I have beaten the Austro-Russian army commanded by the two Emperors. I am a little weary. I have camped in the open for eight days and as many freezing nights. Tomorrow I shall be able to rest in the castle of Prince Kaunitz [at Austerlitz], and I should be able to snatch two or three hours sleep there. The Russian army is not only beaten but destroyed. I embrace you, Napoleon.' Then he turned to his green-draped camp bed, and slept the sleep of the just, watched over by his bodyguard, the Mameluke Roustam, who slept across the bedroom door.

THE AFTERMATH OF THE BATTLE

Napoleon was up early the next morning. After receiving reports confirming that the foe was in full retreat, prodded occasionally by Prince Murat's cavalry screen, he sat down at his desk and completed the Order of the Day he had started the previous night. It was still based on incomplete knowledge, and the statistics quoted were provisional.

'Austerlitz, *12 frimaire, an XIV.*

'Soldiers, I am pleased with you! You have, on this day of Austerlitz, justified all that I had expected from your courage, and you have honoured your eagles with immortal glory. In less than four hours an army of 100,000 men [sic], commanded by the Emperors of Russia and Austria, has been cut down or scattered. Such enemy as escaped your bayonets have drowned in the lakes.

'Forty colours, the standards of the Russian Imperial Guard, 120 pieces of artillery, twenty generals and over 30,000 prisoners are the result of this day – to be for ever celebrated. That such vaunted infantry, so superior in numbers, could not resist your charge, proves that henceforth you have no longer any rivals to fear. Thus in two months this Third Coalition has been overthrown and dissolved. Peace cannot now be far away, but, as I promised my people before crossing the Rhine, I will only make a peace that both gives us guarantees and also assures rewards for our allies. . . . May all the blood shed here, may all these misfortunes, fall upon the heads of the perfidious islanders [the British] who have caused them. May the cowardly oligarchs of London pay the consequences of so many woes.

'Soldiers, when the French people placed the imperial crown upon my head. I trusted in you to sustain it in that high state of glory that alone gives it value in my eyes. But at that very moment our foes were planning to destroy and debase it, together with the Iron Crown [of the Kingdom of Italy], won by the blood of so many Frenchmen; they wished to compel me to place it upon the head of our greatest foes – bold, senseless plots, which, on the very day of the coronation anniversary, you have confounded and destroyed. You have taught them that it is easier to boast before us and to threaten us than it is to conquer us.

'Soldiers, when everything necessary for the happiness and prosperity of our Motherland has been accomplished, I will lead you back to France: there you will be the object of my tenderest solicitude. My people will greet you with joy, and it will suffice for you to say: "I was at the battle of Austerlitz," for them to reply: "There is one of the brave."

"NAPOLEON".'

Four days later the Emperor would keep his word. Two decrees were promulgated at Austerlitz on 7 December, distributing rewards. Two million gold francs were distributed among the senior officers; general officers received 6,000 francs, colonels and majors 2,400 francs, captains 1,200, lieutenants and second-lieutenants 800, and each soldier was awarded 200 francs. Pensions were to be provided for the widows of the fallen. Orphaned children were formally adopted by the Emperor in person, and permitted to add 'Napoleon' to their baptismal names. All would be found places in the special state schools; boys would be found posts, girls would be found husbands and awarded dowries at state expense.

The memory of Austerlitz was to be kept green forever – and to the present day each 2 December is commemorated at the French Military School of Saint-Cyr Coétiquidian in Brittany by an hour-long re-enactment by the complete body of the Officer Cadets, held on the School's training area, which is called (but of course!) *'Le Pratzen'*. Austerlitz is also the name of a major railway station in Paris. As for the captured cannon, most were melted down and used to reinforce the Colonne Vendôme in one of the capital's main squares – where it stands today.

But one commemorative honour Napoleon refused to bestow. When, in 1808, the time came for the bestowal of dukedoms and other distinctions on the Marshalate, Jean-Nicolas Soult suggested that he should be created 'Duke of Austerlitz'. Napoleon refused. There could be 'Dukes of Rivoli', 'Auerstädt', and (later) Princes 'of Wagram' and 'of the Moscowa' – but there should never be a 'Duke' or 'Prince of Austerlitz'. That was one title Napoleon was determined to reserve, unused, for himself.

Later on the 3rd, Napoleon wrote a short letter to his elder brother, Joseph. 'Although I have bivouaced in the open air these eight days past, my health is nevertheless good. This evening I shall sleep in a bed at the fine castle of Monsieur de Kaunitz at Austerlitz – something I haven't been able to do for a week.' The Emperor – despite the legend – was not wholly averse to the basic comforts of life.

In the meantime details of the scale of the victory – and of its cost – were being diligently assembled by the Emperor's secretaries. When all was known, or thought to be, it appeared that the Allies had lost nine generals, twenty senior commanders, and 800 more junior officers. The casualties were split between the Allies as follows: of the dead, 11,000 were Russian and 4,000 were Austrian. Some details are available, but rather suspect. The official Russian returns (exclusive of the Imperial Guard Corps except for its heavy cavalry) admit to 19,886 cavalry and infantry lost, and 3,616 gunners. The 18 convoys of prisoners trudging through Brünn on their way to the Rhine comprised 9,767 Russians and 1,686 Austrians. The Imperial Guard's losses are still unknown – but must have been considerable, the Chevalier Guards alone losing 200 prisoners of war. The number of Austrian dead was about 600. As for booty, besides the 186 guns, the French had captured 45 regimental colours (to be sent in due course to decorate the cathedral of Notre-Dame), 400 artillery caissons and all the army's heavy baggage – besides many thousand Russian knapsacks.

The French losses were declared in round numbers to be 1,300 killed, 7,000 wounded, and 573 taken prisoner by the enemy. Friant's 1st Division of III Corps had suffered worst, having lost 1,900 men; next came Saint-Hilaire's 1st Division with 1,776, then Vandamme's 2nd Division with 1,456 – both formations of IV Corps. The casualties suffered by I Corps were very light, possibly reflecting the rather insipid role it had played thanks to Bernadotte's caution – some would say (and did at the time) over-caution. Many statistics are unreliable, but it would appear that one of the units that fared worst was the *24ème Légère* Regiment of General Schinner's Brigade in Vandamme's Division, which lost 126 killed and 364 wounded. One general (Valhubert), 3 staff and 87 other officers were among the slain or died of

Reception of French wounded at Vienna, by Gros. Many of the French wounded were sent to hospitals at Brünn but several convoys of the stricken were sent back to Vienna, where the citizens, forgetting enmity, did their best to succour them. (Anne S. K. Brown Military Collection, Brown University)

wounds, and 13 generals, 32 staff and 460 more junior officers lay among the wounded.

The meeting between the French and Austrian Emperors took place at 2pm on 4 December at the appointed rendezvous. A large bonfire had been lit, and a simple plank attached to a fallen tree-trunk served as a seat. Francis II arrived in a carriage accompanied by Prince Lichtenstein, escorted by two squadrons. Napoleon had deployed the entire Imperial Guard in full parade dress on a ridge overlooking the scene. Over the valley were drawn up parts of the Austrian army. The Emperor Francis, looking far older than his 36 years, refused Napoleon's preferred embrace as he stepped from his carriage, but then spoke a few genial words which helped break the ice. The discussions lasted for about two hours. What was actually said is not known, but some laughter was observed, and when they parted Francis looked more cheerful than when he arrived – and allowed the demonstrative Napoleon to hug him. Thus met for the first time the two men who were destined in five years' time to

Central Europe after the Peace of Pressburg

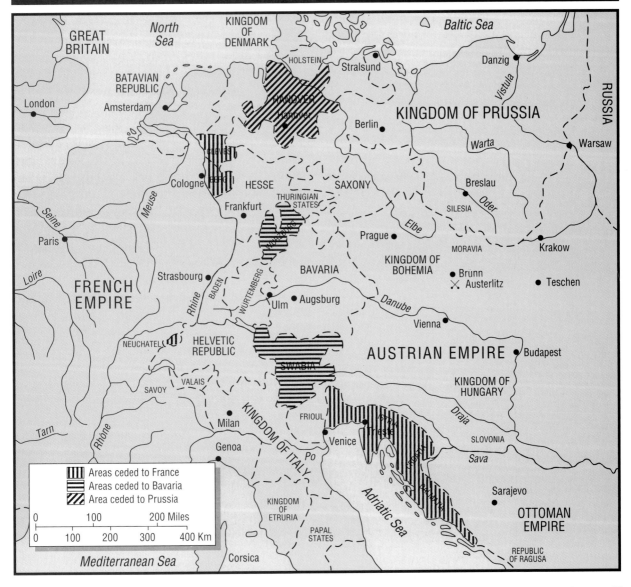

Areas ceded to France
Areas ceded to Bavaria
Area ceded to Prussia

become son- and father-in-law. No doubt what had pleased Francis II was Napoleon's agreement to grant an armistice to come into effect on the 5th.

As Napoleon wrote later to his foreign minister, Talleyrand, at Vienna, 'The Emperor of Austria asked for an interview, which I granted; it lasted from 2 until 4pm. I will tell you what I think of him when I see you. He wished to conclude peace on the spot. He appealed to my feelings; I defended myself – a kind of warfare which I assure you was not difficult. He asked me for an armistice, which I conceded. . . . Inform the Austrians that the battle has changed the face of affairs and that they must expect harder conditions; that I complain, above all, of their conduct in sending me negotiators on the day they intended to attack me, in order to throw me off my guard. . . . You will tell M. Haugwitz [the Prussian Foreign Minister who had been sent from Brünn before the battle] to wait for me in Vienna.' In this last phrase lay the seeds of a future war, for Napoleon was going to exact a merciless revenge for King Frederick William III's near-joining of the Third Coalition. As Napoleon cryptically remarked when he at last granted Haugwitz an audience, the fulsome congratulations being expressed 'appear to have been recently readdressed'.

The meeting of Napoleon and Francis, after Gros. On 4 December, near the village of Urchutz, Napoleon meets the Emperor Francis, who had come to seek an armistice. The interview lasted an hour. Prince

John of Lichtenstein was also present at the conference, at which the Habsburg emperor solemnly undertook not to recommence hostilities. (Anne S. K. Brown Military Collection, Brown University)

The French pursuit meanwhile was only sporadically conducted, and when General Savary arrived at Göding with news of the forthcoming armistice late on the 4th he found hostilities had already ceased by what appeared to be mutual agreement. Napoleon's chief of intelligence lingered to see the Russians march over a bridge on their way towards Hungary and Poland, and calculated their strength at 'no more than 26,000. . . all arms included. Most of them had lost their knapsacks, and a great many were wounded but they marched bravely in their ranks.' The stoicism of the Russian soldiers had already earned the grudging admiration of the French army. The Tsar sent a message for onward transmission to Napoleon: 'Tell your master that I am going away. Tell him that he has performed miracles. . . that the battle has increased my admiration for him; that he is a man predestined by Heaven; that it will require a hundred years for my army to equal his.'

In these words were spelt the doom of William Pitt's Third Coalition. When news of Austerlitz reached London, the Prime Minister ordered his servants to 'roll up that map of Europe. We shall not need it these seven years.' Meanwhile in Vienna three weeks of intensive negotiation ensued. The result was the Peace of Pressburg, signed on 26 December. As was to be expected, the terms were harsh (see map). Austria was compelled to cede Venice to swell the new Napoleonic Kingdom of Italy; the Tyrol, Vorarlberg and other Alpine territories were torn away to be awarded to the faithful French ally, Bavaria; the Duke of Württemberg received Swabia. Pitt's glum comment about the map of Europe was all too apt: a period of immense cartographical adjustment at the dictation of a victorious France was about to begin, and it would not be returned to something approaching its pre-1805 frontiers until after Waterloo in 1815. Not that the brilliant British Premier would see that day. The renewed shattering of all his hopes represented by Austerlitz proved too much for his frail constitution, already gravely weakened by undue recourse to the bottle. Within a few weeks (in January 1806) Napoleon's most inveterate opponent would, broken-hearted, turn his face to the wall and die. Napoleon was well on the way to becoming the master of Europe.

CHRONOLOGY

Events leading up to the Battle of Austerlitz
16 May 1803 Great Britain declares war on the French Republic.
15 June 1803 *L'Armée d'Angleterre* forms the Camp of Boulogne on the Channel.
13 February 1804 Failure of the Cadoudal plot against the First Consul's life.
14 March 1804 The kidnapping of the Duc d'Enghien at Ettenheim.
21 March 1804 Execution of the Duc d'Enghien at Vincennes.
16 August 1804 Presentation of *Légions d'Honneur* at Boulogne.
11 April 1804 The Third Coalition starts to come into existence.
18 May 1804 Napoleon proclaimed Emperor after a plebiscite.
2 December 1804 Napoleon crowned Emperor at Notre Dame in Paris.
26 May 1805 Napoleon crowned King of Italy in Milan.
9 August 1805 The Third Coalition completed by the adherence of Austria.
20 August 1805 Admiral Villeneuve takes shelter with Franco-Spanish Fleet in Cadiz.
25 August 1805 Napoleon orders the abandonment of the Camp of Boulogne (completed on 3 September) and heads for the Rhine.
10 September 1805 Austrian General Mack occupies Ulm, following the invasion of Bavaria.
24 September 1805 *La Grande Armée d'Allemagne* begins to cross the Rhine into Germany.
8 October 1805 French win the Combat of Wertingen.
11 October 1805 General Dupont wins Action of Haslach.
14 October 1805 Marshal Ney wins Action of Elchingen. Mack withdraws last forces into Ulm.
20 October 1805 Surrender of Mack's army at Ulm.

21 October 1805 Franco-Spanish fleet destroyed off Cape Trafalgar; death of Lord Nelson.
26 October 1805 Napoleon launches the pursuit of General Kutusov's Russian army.
28 October 1805 Marshal Massena fights Battle of Caldiero in North Italy (until 31st).
11 November 1805 Isolated French force wins Action of Durrenstein on north bank of Danube.
12 November 1805 Prince Murat occupies Vienna and captures the major bridge by bluff.
15 November 1805 General Bagration fools Murat into an armistice at Hollabrünn.
16 November 1805 French break armistice; Battle of Hollabrünn ensues.
20 November 1805 Kutusov joins Buxhöwden and Tsar Alexander I near Olmütz.
23 November 1805 Napoleon halts the French pursuit at Brünn.
30 November 1805 French troops abandon Austerlitz and the Pratzen Heights to lure the foe.
1 December 1805 The rival armies take up their battle positions. Marshal Bernadotte and I Corps arrive from Iglau; Marshal Davout's leading elements of III Corps are approaching from Vienna.
2 December 1805 THE BATTLE OF AUSTERLITZ.

Timing of Events on 2 December 1805

1am Allied staff conference ends.
1.30am Napoleon completes 'torchlight' procession.
2am Sharp skirmish at Sokolnitz.
4am French go to battle stations in fog.
7am Buxhöwden's three columns attack Sokolnitz and Telnitz.
8.30am Allies capture villages; General Friant (III Corps) checks them, Buxhöwden summons Kollowrath from the Pratzen Heights.

9am Soult's IV Corps occupies the near-abandoned Pratzen Heights.
10am Lannes' V Corps and Murat's Cavalry Reserve repulse Bagration and Prince Lichtenstein on the French left wing.
12am Soult completes occupation of the Pratzen plateau. Napoleon moves to Staré Vinohrady feature with the Imperial Guard, Oudinot's Grenadiers and part of Bernadotte's I Corps.
1pm Russian Imperial Guard counter-attacks IV Corps. Early progress reversed by French Imperial Guard cavalry and part of I Corps.
2pm Napoleon moves IV Corps southwards, supported by Guard and Oudinot.
2.30pm III Corps counter-attacks Buxhöwden. Allied left wing begins withdrawal.
3pm Part of Allied left escapes from Napoleon's trap: part destroyed on or near the frozen meres.
4pm Allied rout completed. Bagration's wing retreats. Heavy snow halts fighting.

Events following the Battle of Austerlitz

3 December 1805 The Emperor Francis I appeals for an interview. French occupy Austerlitz as pursuit begins.
4 December 1805 Interview between Napoleon and Francis I. An armistice is agreed. Allies march towards Hungary to regroup, but Russians soon head for Poland.
26 December 1805 Peace of Pressburg concluded.
26 January 1806 Napoleon reaches Paris.

A GUIDE TO FURTHER READING

On the **place of the events** of 1805 within the Napoleonic Wars: Chandler, D. G., *The Campaigns of Napoleon*, New York & London, 1967.

On the campaign and battle of Austerlitz, useful for the **Allied** view: Duffy, C. J., *Austerlitz*, London, 1977. Includes a good bibliography.

On the campaign and battle of Austerlitz, useful for the **French** view: Manceron, C., *Austerlitz*, Paris & London, 1962 & 1966. Light-weight. Ponod, A., *Austerlitz*, Paris, 1954. Biased, but reasonably accurate. Alombert P. and Colin J., *La Campagne de 1805 en Allemagne*, Paris 1902–8; a massive documentation, but incomplete, as it ends in mid-November.

On the **French Army**, its organization, equipment, tactics etc: Elting, J., *Swords around the Throne*, New York and London, 1988. Excellent. Haythornthwaite, P. J., *Napoleon's Military Machine*, London, 1988. Good.

Atlas: Esposito, V. J., and Elting, J. R., *A Military History and Atlas of the Napoleonic Wars*, New York and London, 1964, 1978, 1980.

General Reference on the period: Chandler, D. G., *Dictionary of the Napoleonic Wars*, New York and London, 1969. Comprehensive.

Best Contemporary Accounts:
Fairon, E., and Heuse H., *Lettres des Grognards*, Paris, 1936.
Rapp, J., *The Memoirs of General Rapp*, English edition), London, 1840.
Savary, A. J. M. R., *Les Mémoirs du Duc de Rovigo*, 8 volumes, Paris, 1828.
Stutterheim, General, *A Detailed Account of the Battle of Austerlitz*, (reprinted) Cambridge, 1985. The best Austrian account.
Thiébault, P. C. F., *Mémoirs du Général Baron Thiébault*, 3 volumes, Paris 1894. The best French source.
Wilson, R., *Brief Remarks on the Character and Composition of the Russian Army*, London, 1810.

The incomparable fictional account:
Tolstoy, L., *War and Peace*, London, 1972 (and many other editions). The first half.

THE BATTLEFIELD TODAY

At the present time the battlefield of Austerlitz remains largely unchanged since 1805. However, it is also clear that the suburbs of Brno (the modern form of Brünn) are advancing remorselessly towards the Santon – which may cause problems for the historically-minded visitor in the medium-to-long term. The existence of a thriving if still small Napoleonic Re-enactment Society may help stave off possible disaster, especially as Czechoslovakia in the age of *glasnost* and *perestroika* is becoming increasingly aware of the advantages of encouraging visitors from other countries throughout the world, and with this has come a growing perception of the importance of preserving such significant battlefields as Austerlitz, Kolin and Sadowa as, at the very least, tourist attractions.

Starting from the railway station in Brno, a drive of six miles along the road E7 towards Olmütz will bring the visitor to the Zurlan hill. A small road leads off to the right to the summit where a stone plinth holds a bronze (and hence practically vandal-proof) relief map of the early-morning positions of the rival armies. This is an excellent orientation point, and one gets two main impressions: first of the overall extent of the battlefield area (twice as large as Waterloo – perhaps five miles north to south – although only some 179,600 men of all sides were present as compared to all of 262,000, to include Blücher's three corps, at the battle of 18 June 1815); and second of the relatively gentle slope of the Pratzen Heights on the western side (although this is more pronounced close-to) from the Goldbach stream – only the distant southern cliffs presenting much of a strong topographical feature. The Pratzen is surmounted by a large memorial – taking the form of a crucifix atop a sloping cone. Away to the north the tree-clad feature of the Santon can be picked out with its chapel spire, and beyond it the higher feature of the Goldbach Heights. Away to the east is the village of

Koválovice, where a small chapel was built to commemorate the Russian dead and is worth a visit in its sylvan setting if time allows.

To reach the Santon you need to return to the E7 and continue east before turning left towards Tvarozná (Bosenitz). At the western end of the village a track leads towards the Santon – and a steepish climb through trees brings you to the chapel on the summit (a building dating from 1832: the original was demolished during the preparations for battle on 1 December 1805). Unfortunately the trees obliterate the view to a large extent, but note the precipitous northern side, which faced towards Bagration's right wing of the Allied army and presented a daunting obstacle to a would-be attacker. A battery of cannon is also on the site.

Return to the E7 and take the first turning to the left after the road leading up the Zurlan to Bedrichovice (Bellowitz) and Slapanice (Schlappanitz or Lapanz Markt), where refreshment can be found. (The Czechs are very fond of suet dumplings – and delicious they can be with a good gravy sauce.) In Slapanice be sure to visit the castle, or rather stately school today, which served as Soult's headquarters and the main French military hospital in 1805 after the battle. You are now approaching the valley of the Goldbach, which is full of orchards, and it was the clear reverse slopes here that concealed the presence of Bernadotte's I Corps and Murat's Reserve Cavalry from Allied telescopes. Bernadotte's headquarters were in what is now a small museum, originally a church school, in Lapanz Markt.

Moving towards Puntowitz (Ponetovice) you are passing over Saint-Hilaire's and Vandamme's forming-up area, screened on 2 December 1805 by the lingering fog. The road now begins to climb up towards the low saddle of the central Pratzen Heights, and follows the precise line of advance of

Saint-Hilaire's Division to the village of Prace (Pratzen). Near this small hamlet with its rebuilt church (1810) a road leads off north-west towards Bläswitz (Blazovice) which, after some 450 yards, brings you to the Staré Vinohrady feature – Napoleon's second command post was here. From this natural vantage point the main panorama of the battlefield is stretched before you. Blazovice (Bläswitz) and the area held by Prince Lichtenstein's cavalry lie to the north; back over the Pratzen saddle to the south is the scene of the Allied Fourth Column's battle against Soult's IV Corps. The earlier meeting between Tsar Alexander I and General Kutusov probably took place where the secondary road to Blazovice branches away to the left, although this is not firmly established. Given the vastness of the general area it is clear that the rival formations must have been very spread out over the ground indeed.

To visit the Battle Memorial and Grave return to Prace village and a short distance up the steep road to its south. It was built in 1912 and contains a sealed crypt full of human bones found on the battlefield, and a small chapel which has a strange echo and a skeleton in a glass coffin – much the same as the one displayed at Le Caillou Farm in Belgium. A good museum also contains dioramas and relics of the battle. Looking west, the lower reaches of the Goldbach can be discerned by the sharp-eyed, and very clear is the thick clump of trees which is the Sokolnitz (Sokolnice) pheasantry. Due south and out of sight is Újezd (Aujest Markt), scene of the French attempt to seal Buxhöwden's line of retreat, but this is better visited from valley of the Velatick'y potok (Goldbach Stream) as a Soviet radar-station stands in a hollow above the village and on the north-east side of the Pratzen Heights, near which Napoleon's third (and final) command-post, the Chapel of St Anthony (now completely disappeared).

Driving out of Prace (Pratzen) in a westerly direction to Kobyllnice (Kobelnitz) and then farther west towards Turany (Turas), stop at the top of the first rise beyond Kobelnitz. Before you is the scene of the destruction of the Allied Third Column. It will be noted that the ponds that existed here in 1805 have long since been drained. Returning south through Kobyllnice, you will soon find on your right a low wall containing part of the Sokolnitz pheasantry. Nearer that village, do not miss the five crosses cut into the wall showing the exact positions of a French battery in 1805. The castle of Sokolnitz is today a yellow-walled country house and part of a factory. Much of the present town and industrial area is, of course, modern.

The Goldbach Stream is little more than a ditch today, but driving south we come to Telnice (Telnitz). The vineyards and gardens line the sheltering low bank, which saw much fighting by light infantry in 1805. Carrying on through Satcany (Satschan) to Ujezd (Aujest Markt) you are close to the sites of the drained Satschn and Menitz meres, which have now long-since been drained to make more arable land, but the dominating southern cliffs of the Pratzen Heights are quite clear here.

Following the line of the Litava (Liiawa) valley, you will in due course reach Slavkov (Austerlitz). Do not fail to visit the museum in the castle of Prince Kaunitz (where Napoleon at last found a bed indoors on 3 December, and where rather more recently, in August 1989, a re-enactment was held, which brought together parties of uniformed soldiery from Great Britain, Belgium, France, West Germany and – uniquely – from the Soviet Union. The castle contains a museum of maps and prints relating to December 1805. Returning from Slavkov towards Brno, take time to turn right when you rejoin the E7 for a few hundred yards along on the left (as you face east) is the Pozorická posta – or Pozorice post-house, where Napoleon dried off and took supper before being visited by Prince Lichtenstein at a very late hour on 2 December 1805 with a request for a summit meeting with Francis II.

A reasonably complete visit to the battlefield and area in a car or coach requires a full day; a minimum visit needs three hours. A good map is desirable (for example Czechoslavakia, Series GSGS 4741 (1/25,000), Sheet 686) together with a compass and binoculars. Cameras are not frowned upon but common-sense must be used as to subjects chosen.

WARGAMING AUSTERLITZ

Choosing to wargame Austerlitz, as with any historical rather than hypothetical or fictitious scenario, raises some pertinent questions about the players' objectives, which must be resolved before the game is designed. Is the original campaign to be used merely as a starting point, so that the players' subsequent decisions can alter history, or is the intention to recreate the historical manoeuvres and engagements as accurately as possible? Is there to be a series of wargames, each covering a different aspect of the campaign, or only one? How many players will be taking part? What roles do they wish to play – the Emperors and their staffs, corps commanders, regimental officers or humble infantrymen? Only when the participants have decided exactly what they want will they be able to choose or design an appropriate game to satisfy their expectations; unlike so many other games or sports, in wargaming there is no one universally accepted game structure or set of rules!

For the purpose of these suggestions, it is assumed that readers may wish to play a series of games recreating various facets of the Austerlitz campaign, or to select those which reflect the interest aroused by reading this book. The 1805 campaign seems to be characterized by sweeping strategic manoeuvres, methodical staffwork on one side and internal dissension on the other, culminating in a climactic battle. Outlines of wargames that attempt to recreate these characteristics are described below.

'Roll Up That Map' – The Manoeuvre of Ulm

William Pitt's remark may not be an inappropriate title for a strategic wargame that will inevitably involve maps. Since no wargamer could be relied upon to be as supine as the 'unhappy General Mack' – especially once he knows that the Austerlitz campaign is the scenario! – an 'open', face-to-face boardgame is unlikely to provide a satisfactory recreation. One solution to the hindsight problem is to disguise the scenario, with player briefings set in an alternative historical, or even completely fictitious, background. This would require considerable work by the game organizer, and there would be no guarantee that players would not penetrate the disguise or deviate from the historical manoeuvres so that the resulting campaign bore only the most superficial resemblance to the original. It would be preferable to concentrate upon recreating the French experience of the march to Ulm, while an umpire controlled the Austrians, allowing the game design to introduce logistics, reconnaissance and detailed staffwork.

One option would be to play Imperial Headquarters; players would take the roles of Napoleon, Berthier and Bacler d'Albe, study maps, issue orders to the umpires, and receive written reports, or personal visits, from subordinates. The latter would be role-played by assistant umpires, after being briefed by the umpires around a master map on which the current positions of all French and Allied formations were recorded. The umpires would use simple rules to determine the distance covered in a day's march by each corps, adjusted to reflect the troops' fatigue and the availability of food, the state of the roads, including congestion caused by stragglers and baggage wagons, and the weather. The objective would be to recreate the atmosphere of Napoleon's Headquarters on campaign; the emphasis would be upon decision-making and paperwork, rather than leadership in battle.

A second option would be to play the Emperor and all his corps commanders in a large map game or kriegsspiel. Each game turn would represent a day, at the start of which players would issue orders to the umpires, who would then resolve their implementation on the master map, return situation reports and messages during the turn to players and control the Austrians in accordance with history. There would obviously be less detailed re-creation of staffwork than in the previous game, but more players would be able to participate and the umpires' workload reduced since they would no longer have to generate some of the correspondence. This game could be played by distributing players around a house or community hall, out of sight and earshot of each other, with a rigid time limit for receipt of orders each turn and stylised, boardgame-type rules for movement and combat on the master map; or over a period of time by post and telephone. A particularly suitable system for such a game, which requires players to plan their day's activity so as to ensure that each commander allows time to write orders and despatches, visit his troops, take exercise, eat and sleep, is to be found in Paddy Griffith's *Napoleonic Wargaming for Fun*.

Yet another option would be to play a similar game set within one corps. Napoleon's historical orders would be issued by the umpires, whereupon the Marshal would have to brief his division commanders and check that his orders were obeyed correctly. At this level more detailed consideration of logistics, the troops' health and morale, orders of march, traffic jams and the state of the roads would be possible than in either of the two previous games. Other French corps would be controlled by umpires and conform to their original movements.

All these games require maps. Ideally, the game designer should endeavour to obtain photocopies of suitable contemporary maps, which would add to the atmosphere of the game and give players a greater appreciation of one of the hazards of early nineteenth century campaigning! Alternatively, a modern map could be redrawn with appropriate omissions and embellishments. In a highly stylised game, such as the 'generalship game' referred to above, a schematic diagram along the lines of the London Underground map, where each 'stop' is a town or city a day's march from the next, rather than an accurate-scale map, would be suitable. In all these games the umpires should, if possible, have more detailed maps than the players, from which they can take information to create reconnaissance reports or describe the results of personal observation.

On the March

As a counterpoint to the rarified atmosphere of Imperial or Corps Headquarters, why not create a game to illustrate the daily hardships of the *fantassin* discovering that 'The Emperor . . . makes use of our legs instead of our bayonets . . .', worrying about his disintegrating shoes, the fact that he has not been paid for weeks and where his next meal is coming from? This would be portrayed in a short, free-form roleplay, in which the umpire would present the player with a series of decision points, in the manner of the popular *Fighting Fantasy* gamebooks. Success will be arriving on the outskirts of Ulm, footsore but in high spirits, with a knapsack full of plunder, having sampled both the local brew and the willing wenches; failure will be falling out, to die of exhaustion or dysentery by the roadside. . . .

To prepare such a game, the umpire should immerse himself in contemporary accounts and historical novels, which will be full of incidents he can incorporate into the narrative. R. F. Delderfield's *Seven Men of Gascony* would be an excellent starting point.

The Battle of Elchingen

A series of wargames of the Austerlitz campaign would not be complete without a recreation of the battle that gained Marshal Ney the title of Duc d'Elchingen. This is the one engagement of the campaign where the number of troops engaged is small enough to be represented without having to adopt ludicrous model-soldier: man ratios, and the battle took place in a confined area, which can be recreated on the wargame table. Although Ney's VI Corps outnumbered the Austrian defenders of Elchingen – the corps of Reisch and Werneck – by nearly three to one, only Dupont's Division was on the north bank of the Danube, and Ney had to lead the 6th Regiment of Loison's Division across an almost demolished bridge under heavy fire before assaulting the town of Elchingen and its large abbey on the steep ridge beyond the river. The battle raged for three hours before the arrival of Mahler's Division, which had crossed the Danube farther to the east, forced the Austrians to withdraw. For much of the game, therefore, the French numerical superiority will not be so great, and will be somewhat outweighed by the strength of the Austrian position.

Elchingen may be refought using figures in any of the popular wargame sizes – 6, 15 or 25mm – but the smaller-scale models would be cheaper, easier to paint and could be used *en masse* to create a more realistic visual appearance. The Austrian players should be allowed to study the town and its surroundings before the game so that they can plan their deployment. Incidentally, a perfectly adequate terrain for wargames may be created by spreading a thick green cloth over some books and old clothes and indicating roads and rivers with appropriately coloured chalks or strips of ribbon, completing the scene with some model buildings (easily constructed from plastic or card kits intended for model railways, or scratch-built from waste materials) to represent the town and some trees or clumps of lichen (also obtainable from model railway suppliers) the forest behind it. The Austrians should then place on the table only those troops that would be visible to Ney from the opposite bank of the Danube and note the positions of units hidden inside or behind buildings on a diagram. Ney then deploys his forces and the game commences. Hidden Austrian units will only be placed on the table when they open fire or the French move to a position from which they would be visible. Mahler's Division will only appear on the eastern edge of the table after a number of game turns equivalent to three and a half hours has been played. There are several commercial sets of rules for Napoleonic battle games, most of which would probably give a satisfactory game; the players must simply experiment until they find a set they find corresponds to their interpretation of the reality of battle and is easy to use.

The Advance to Austerlitz

There is little that need be said about gaming *la Grande Armée*'s movements after the capitulation of Ulm; any of the games described under the heading 'Roll Up That Map' will be found equally suitable to re-create this period of the campaign. An alternative would be to reverse the roles and play Kutusov and Buxhöwden, the French being umpire-controlled instead. Kutusov's efforts to avoid the French trap and effect a junction with Buxhöwden would certainly provide a challenging map game or kriegsspiel.

Council of War at Olmütz Castle

As a change from strategic map games and tactical figure games, the game organizer may care to set up a committee game of the Allied command discussions in the days immediately before Austerlitz. Each player takes an individual role – Alexander, Francis, Kutusov, Weyrother, Czartoryski or Dolgorouki – and receives a personal briefing detailing his opinions, knowledge and objective, which will usually be to win the whole council of war, or named individuals, over to his viewpoint (although in Kutusov's case it might simply be to curtail the discussion so he can return to his wenches and his bottle). The Tsar, in particular, will be anxious to maintain the dignity of his rank and not be seen to defer to his generals; Russian officers will despise the Austrians after the humiliation of Ulm; and so on.

Discussion may be limited to a certain time, at the end of which the game organizer will determine to what extent each player has fulfilled his personal objectives, or until a plan of action has been agreed. Besides allowing the players to display their debating skills, this game will illustrate vividly the internal conflicts and dissension that plagued the Allied Headquarters.

'Le Beau Soleil d'Austerlitz': 2 December 1805

The climax of the series of games would be the Battle of the Three Emperors. There are several problems that must be overcome, not the least of which is that of hindsight: if the players were simply presented with the historical deployments and then left to their own devices, the resulting battle would be extremely unlikely to resemble the historical Austerlitz in anything but name! Therefore, both sides must be forced to adhere to their original orders. The extent of the battlefield, and the number of troops involved, would be difficult to represent using the larger wargame figures and inordinately time-consuming if conventional brigade- or division-level rules were employed. Nor would an 'open', face-to-face boardgame recreate the inability of the commanders on either side to see the entire battlefield.

One method of gaming Austerlitz would be to stage a large, multi-player kriegsspiel. Each player would command a corps and sit separately with an individual copy of a detailed map of the battlefield, covered with transparent plastic, upon which he may mark with washable marker pens the positions of his own and such enemy troops as he can see. Orders will be sent to the umpires, who will note the positions of all troops on their master map and inform the players of the results of combats, the current positions of their troops, and describe what they can see of the enemy. Any communication between players must be by note delivered via the umpires, unless they have moved to the same location on the battlefield. Commanders-in-chief might remain with their reserve, or visit their corps commanders to observe the situation in that part of the field for themselves by consulting the players' individual maps. The umpires would have to impose appropriate delays to allow for the time spent riding from one corps to another. There are, at present, no published kriegsspiel rules for army-level action, so the game organizer will have to devise his own guidelines for umpires.

If the game organizer is determined to use model soldiers he would have to adopt a radically different game system from that of typical recreational wargames. One idea that has been tried in a megagame (a wargame with more than thirty players) of the battle of Novi was to use 25mm figures on the floor of a large hall, each player controlling a regiment or brigade and issuing orders chosen from a simple menu, such as 'Form Line', 'Open Fire', 'Charge' and so on, to an umpire team on a pro-forma each turn. Orders for each army had previously been issued by those playing the commanders: for Austerlitz one would use the historical orders. The umpires moved the troops and resolved musketry and bayonet charges according to a simple set of rules specially designed for the game, and returned the pro-forma to the players at the end of each turn with details of casualties and morale. In order to succeed, such a game requires large numbers of model soldiers and very efficient umpiring indeed to maintain the pace of combat.

Another option would be to use small figures and boardgame-style combat resolution at brigade or division level by assigning a numerical combat value to each unit and comparing the results when modified by a die score and one or two tactical factors. The battlefield would be divided into zones, each of which would be represented by a model terrain on a separate table so that the entire battlefield could not be seen from any one vantage point. Commanders-in-chief would be able to travel from one zone to another, subject to delays and the hazards of stray shots, as in the kriegsspiel described above.

Yet another possibility is a simulator that attempts to re-create a perspective view of the battlefield from the commander's vantage point. Napoleon's position remained static for much of the battle, so it may be possible to draw a perspective view upon which sketches of bodies of troops, increasing in size as they approach and decreasing as they retire, would be moved by umpires. So far, manual simulators have tended to be confined to portraying only one side in a small action, but there is already a computer simulation of Borodino, so the technique may become more widely used in future. The technology and programing skills required to create such a game are probably beyond the reach of most wargamers at present, but this may be the shape of wargames to come.